WHEN GOVERNMENTS LISTEN

NATIONAL CENTER FOR CIVIC INNOVATION

Also by Barbara J. Cohn Berman

*Listening to the Public: Adding the Voices of the People to Government
Performance Measurement and Reporting (2005)*

WHEN GOVERNMENTS LISTEN

Moving Toward Publicly Engaged Governing

Barbara J. Cohn Berman
National Center for Civic Innovation
Center on Government Performance

The National Center for Civic Innovation
is an Affiliate of the
Fund for the City of New York
121 Avenue of the Americas
New York, NY 10013

Library of Congress Control Number: 2012937108
ISBN 978-0-9768490-3-2

Graphic Design, Kathryn Weinstein

With immense gratitude, we acknowledge the Alfred P. Sloan Foundation for providing long-standing support of the work of the Center on Government Performance.

"If you listen to the citizens, they will give you enormous feedback as to whether your data are even measuring what you need to be measuring. From feedback from the focus groups, we have reexamined data and found some to be lacking. We also found that we did not offer, in many cases, the data in which the citizens were most interested." (Trailblazer)

CONTENTS

PART FOUR

PART FIVE

TABLES, CHARTS AND ILLUSTRATIONS

        Why did your government apply for the Trailblazer Program?
        Why did you and your government want to be Trailblazers?
        How did you come to be in the role of initiating or sustaining this
        Trailblazer Program?

SYNOPSIS

Since 2003, the Center on Government Performance (CGP) of the National Center for Civic Innovation has operated what has come to be known as the Government Trailblazer Program. This program encourages local and county governments to introduce publicly-informed performance measures and reports into their practices. Since 1995, the Alfred P. Sloan Foundation has supported CGP's work.

Publicly-informed performance measures and reports are produced when local and county governments seek feedback from the public about existing performance measures and reports and then incorporate some or all of the suggestions from the public into subsequent measures, reports and management practices whenever practicable. Beyond that, they adapt publicly- engaged governing practices by developing and institutionalizing non-confrontational means to listen to, respond to and learn from the public so that there is better alignment between government's activities and the public's needs for information and governmental action.

The Government Trailblazer Program was developed by CGP after it introduced market research techniques to discover how the public judges government performance in New York City. The results from several rounds of focus groups have been described in our 2005 book, *Listening to the Public: Adding the Voices of the People to Government Performance Measurement and Reporting.* That research made clear that the public's perspective is different from government's typical measures. For example, people are interested in outcomes and the quality of work performed, regardless of which agency is responsible. Governments, on the other hand, collect information that is often required for accounting, budgeting, workforce planning and other significant and essential purposes. They report information agency by agency.

When performance measures are used by government to assess how it is doing, and those measures are different from the way the public judges government, a major disconnect is the result. This leads to confusion on the part of employees and a low opinion of government by the public.

If, however, governments listen to the public in new ways, learning of their points of view, the facts they want and need, by what standards or measures they judge government performance and why, then governments have the information to make program, policy and management changes to move toward greater alignment of government's work with the public's needs.

In the *Listening to the Public* book, we culled from our research many possible new measures of government performance that reflected the public's point of view and/or their need for information from government. We saw the need for and urged others to replicate our work in other places. We then took our own advice and developed the Government Trailblazer Program, the subject of this companion volume.

CGP has worked with 70 governments in the United States and Canada in its Government Trailblazer Program. Trailblazers had to agree to make their existing performance measures and reports accessible to the public, hear the public's views about them, and incorporate the public's perspective in their next reports and in their management practices.

Shortly after the Trailblazers began listening to the public in new ways, they reported back two types of observations that were surprising to them. They learned that the public is interested in what their government is doing, cares about its government, wants information about government's performance and likes being involved in these consultative processes. Second, they discovered that some of the assumptions their government makes about what people need and want are not always correct. People use different measures, want different information and want it presented in different ways.

To be accepted into our Trailblazer program, candidates were required to have the head of the government endorse and support its participation and designate a person to be responsible for starting, managing and reporting about their initiative.

They reported their progress to us on a quarterly basis and attended expense-paid annual Trailblazer meetings to share their accomplishments and learn from other Trailblazers and CGP. We provided Trailblazer governments with other collegial opportunities to communicate with one another, discussing challenges and their and our advice. We also provided modest financial incentives as well as recognition for their role as innovators in government. Concurrently, we documented their work and the developments of this movement, the findings of which appear in this report.

When the Trailblazers started the program, their performance measures and reports were budget-driven and often highly technical. Some were even more than 500 pages long. They were government-initiated, often used only by government, with little or no public consultation or feedback from the public. Dissemination of the measures and reports to the public was rare. The measures themselves were primarily operating statistics, some inputs and outputs and few, if any, outcome measures. Data were for the city or county as a whole, without the ability to drill down to the neighborhood level.

Trailblazers used one or several methods to hear from the public: focus groups, surveys, a combination of surveys and focus groups, postcard response cards, online surveys, feedback meetings with computerized responses, direct interviews, community conversations and town meetings with professional moderators and social media outreach.

It was not always the case that the head of the government initiated this program. Many Trailblazer project directors were below the top executive level. They typically said, "I wanted to do this and suggested to my government that we do so."

Some of the Trailblazer project directors were relatively new to government and brought the interest of doing something new and the idea of publicly-informed performance measurement, reporting and management with them from graduate classes or professional conferences they had attended.

Trailblazer governments are mostly cities (39) located in 24 different states and in two provinces in Canada. The population of Trailblazer cities ranges from 2.7 million (Toronto, Canada) to 3,500 (Brisbane, CA). Three towns, 16 county governments, two city-counties, six special governmental entities such as commissions, special districts and one Indian Nation tribe, and four state-wide government organizations make up the rest of the 70 Trailblazers involved in this program.

In the eight-year period of this study, 2003-2011, the concentration of Trailblazer project directors shifted from being located mainly in their government's budget, finance and audit sections to working out of the executive offices, reflecting a growing interest on the part of mayors and city and county managers to reach out to, hear from and listen to a wide spectrum of their public.

Trailblazers find that focus group sessions, when managed by professionals, provide useful, actionable information and suggestions that are otherwise unobtainable from satisfaction surveys or in public hearings.

Trailblazers find that citizen satisfaction surveys are useful if exploratory questions can be included to discover why people are or are not satisfied with some government operations; otherwise, erroneous conclusions may result.

Trailblazers learned that the public wants reports without jargon and spin and with good news and bad. They want explanations and context. They want timely information that is relevant to their concerns and designed for them to understand, including graphs, charts and pictures when appropriate. They prefer regular, brief reports about their government's performance with the ability to drill down into specific data.

They want information about the outcomes of government efforts and the quality of the work performed. They do not care which agency is responsible for what—they want the results to be timely and of good quality, and they want services to be delivered in a respectful, responsive manner.

As a result of their outreach and the information they heard from the public, some Trailblazers: produced a publicly-available performance report for the first time; created new performance measures that reflected the public's point of view; eliminated measures that they didn't use or need; included good and bad news with explanations; designed user-friendly reports with context, explanations, charts and graphs; sent reports to their entire population in ways that were economical and appealing; installed their report on their website, enabling users to drill down to neighborhood levels in greater detail; produced shorter reports by subject matter that were issued over the course of a year and instituted ways in which feedback from the public would continue on a regular basis.

Typically, the results of Trailblazers' work have been new, accessible, readable, regularly issued reports containing information and explanations that the public seeks. Additionally, there has been more openness from local governments, more frequent interchanges of ideas between governments and their public, explorations of questions and better understanding by the public of government actions and activities.

Advice from Trailblazers and CGP on a range of topics is included in this volume. One consistent finding of ours is that people form their perceptions of agencies and government itself from the attitude and treatment they receive from the first persons they encounter—the gatekeepers.

The information Trailblazers heard from the public is being used to influence the way governmental policy is made and operations are managed. For example, Trailblazers report that their elected officials now use the outcome data to help make budget and other decisions when previously their decisions were made on a purely political or speculative basis. Operations staff now holds regular sessions to review data that help them learn what programs are working well or not so well and take needed corrective actions. Some use the new measures to identify troublesome trends early enough to make necessary timely changes as well as to improve customer service, assess costs and benefits and determine ways to allocate resources in the public's interest. Expecting and depending upon reliable data has become a practice throughout many levels of government. Trailblazers are instituting ways to assure that their data are and will continue to be accurate and reliable.

In three Trailblazer places—one city and two counties—legislation has been enacted that now requires regular performance reports be produced. In the city, the legislation requires that the public be involved in the process!

We observed that top-level support is necessary but not sufficient to mount and sustain an innovation. An able, interested project director must be in place, too. When there is turnover in either position, the initiative can be in danger unless replacements share the commitment and the ability to continue the work. This leads us to conclude that despite the frequent retort that "no one is indispensable," some people are indispensable to an innovative project in an organization.

When Trailblazers were asked why they chose to be part of the program, their major responses were: it provided the opportunity to include, involve and reach out to the public, and it will enhance their current measures, reports and methods. They reported that they welcomed the challenges of doing something new and worthy. Trailblazers appeared to enjoy the challenges of coming up with creative ways to implement the new program and to see the fruits of their efforts.

Starting up this innovation was time-consuming, beset with trial and error and uncertainty. It involved learning new techniques and tested the project director's skills at working with reluctant colleagues, members of the public they did not know and, for some, with elected officials, for the first time. Despite a myriad of other obstacles too—ranging from decreasing revenues to personnel cutbacks—it took most of the Trailblazers only about one year to start up this program. By the end of their first year, most had heard from the public at least once and were then engaged in revising their performance measures or reports and were feeding back the information to the management teams and legislators who make policy or run operations.

Trailblazer project directors were pleased with and proud of the accomplishments that resulted from being part of the Trailblazer Program and were happy to be part of the program as well. Quotations from Trailblazer project directors abound in this report. We do not disclose the writers' or speakers' names or governments in order to honor our pledge to them that the information they provided would be used for research purposes only and not for identification. The comments below are two of many that are relevant to this observation:

> *"It is a great help to continue to be part of the Trailblazer group or cohort, because it inspires, challenges and reminds us to continue the work of improvement, even when our organizational environment might not always be conducive to continuous improvement in these areas."* (County analyst)

> *"We conducted the three focus groups specifically to address two items: excellent customer service and the content, format and layout of the performance report. This exercise was among the most valuable experiences that I have had in my professional life."* (City budget/finance analyst)

In an effort to understand why some governments chose to not be part of the Trailblazer Program, we sent questionnaires to 2,470 government employees who had received notices about the Trailblazer Program but did not apply to it. It appears that the two elements that best explain why these governments have chosen not to be part of the Trailblazer Program are that there was a lack of interest and support from their top leadership and a lack of interest or conviction on the part of the respondents themselves. They were not sure about the need to and usefulness of listening to the public. And they were not enthusiastic about starting an innovation.

Managing an innovation is stimulating, challenging and attractive to some government employees. It is fraught with difficulties, unwelcome challenges and is unattractive for others.

We found that Trailblazer governments were confronted with the same daunting fiscal conditions as the Non-Trailblazer group, and many of the Trailblazers had similar apprehensions about their ability to reach out to the public and doubts about whether the public would respond in helpful ways. Yet those who participated did not let these concerns stop them.

Recognition of accomplishments bestows government employees with rare public acknowledgement of their work and the encouragement to continue to break new ground. The Trailblazer Program provides such recognition to the worthy project directors and governments that participated in this groundbreaking work.

Public employees also need well-designed, content-filled, goal-defined opportunities to compare notes with their counterparts in other places. They need to share their accomplishments and disappointments, exchange experiences and develop ideas and suggestions in a non-confrontational, non-judgmental, non-commercial setting. Face-to-face meetings and small conferences seem to work best. Webinars and conference calls are less good alternatives.

Providing even small financial incentives to governments and reimbursing travel expenses to attend Trailblazer conferences were additional key elements in mounting and continuing this program.

Financial and other support for the Government Trailblazer Program has come from the Alfred P. Sloan Foundation, the National Center for Civic Innovation and its sister organization, the Fund for the City of New York. The Trailblazer Program was designed and operated by the Center on Government Performance of the National Center for Civic Innovation. The collaboration and partnership of these independent organizations and the 70 Trailblazer governments made this initiative possible. There were no hidden agendas—just a pure dedication to the purposes of the program.

No part of this work would have been possible without the interest of the leaders of the 70 Trailblazer governments: county executives, mayors, city managers, heads of commissions and other governmental entities. They chose to be innovators. Equally essential, the hard work and dedication of the designated project directors who ran the day-to-day operations, often on their own time, reveal the true meaning of public service.

Trailblazers need support and encouragement to continue their work. And we need more Trailblazers in government who realize the importance of government and the public sharing information and points of view that lead to greater understanding and improved performance. The need for the public to have confidence in its government is undeniable in a democracy.

PREFACE

The Government Trailblazer Program, the subject of this volume, was developed by the Center on Government Performance at the National Center for Civic Innovation after it introduced, eight years earlier, market research techniques to discover how the public judges government performance. The results from several rounds of our focus group research have been described in our 2005 book, *Listening to the Public: Adding the Voices of the People to Government Performance Measurement and Reporting*[1]. That research made clear that the public's measures are different from the way government reports about itself. Governments' measures are usually collected agency by agency and are often required for accounting, budgeting, workforce planning and other significant and essential purposes. People, however, are interested in the outcomes and the quality of work performed by their governments, regardless of which agency is responsible. They also care about the way they are treated by government. They expect courtesy, respect, even-handedness and knowledgeable, responsive, accessible government employees.

When measures are used by government to assess how it is doing, and those measures are different from the way the public judges government, a major disconnect is the result, which produces confusion for employees and misunderstandings and poor opinions about government by its public.

We produced a number of publicly-informed performance measures of local government services that were derived from our research. We learned that our findings, which we developed in New York City, resonated in cities, counties, and provinces in other places in this country and beyond. We urged other nonprofit organizations and governments themselves to replicate our work elsewhere and introduce systematic and careful research as a new management practice. We

---

[1] Barbara Cohn Berman, *Listening to the Public: Adding the Voices of the People to Government Performance Measurements and Reports,* Fund for the City of New York, New York, 2005.

suggested this so that governments can listen to the public in new ongoing, non-confrontational ways, learning of their points of view, the information they want and need and by what standards or measures they judge government performance and why. Then governments will have the information and, one hopes, the motivation to improve relationships with the public, providing information that the public needs, in ways they can access and understand it, and introducing practices, policies and measures that resonate with the public. Instead of the current situation in which the public often feels powerless[2] and government employees feel unappreciated and misunderstood, a more informed, appreciative populace and a publicly engaged government is the result.

The Government Trailblazer Program came about as a result of our work described in the *Listening to the Public* book. Heeding our own advice to encourage replication of our work elsewhere, we mounted the Trailblazer Program described here to extend those lessons and publicly engaged governing practices to 70 local, county, state and regional governments in the U.S. and Canada. The Trailblazer Program began as a demonstration grant program in 2003. It affords these governments the opportunity to consider whether the ways in which they have been gauging and reporting about their work is relevant to the public's needs, to make changes in both their measures and reports and also in the way they communicate with the public, establishing productive ways to keep communications flowing back and forth between governments and their public in the future.

If we want this development to thrive, we need insight into which levels and types of government officials and governments are inclined to consider initiating, sustaining and using publicly-informed performance measures and reports, what circumstances are necessary and sufficient to start and sustain these practices and what conditions discourage their development or derail it.

We write this report to provide some answers to these questions, using the

---

[2] Cohn Berman, page 9.

voices of the government program directors who undertook this challenge. We call them Trailblazers. They submitted regular status reports to us, answered our questionnaires, participated in interviews with us and attended Trailblazer conferences at which they reported and we recorded the key points of their small group discussions. We draw from those sources along with our observations of the project directors who, over time, represented 70 Trailblazer governments that joined the program. We also reached out to 69 governments and their representatives who chose not to join the program but who answered our survey questions. In effect, we conducted action research, gathering information as the program itself was being honed and operated over an eight-year period.

Quotations from Trailblazer's reports and presentations abound in this publication. We think that their words convey their stories best. We do not, however, disclose the writer's or speaker's name or government and use their generic titles only to honor our pledge to them that the information they provided would be used for research purposes only and not for identification or attribution. We doubt that we would have been able to report their candid comments had we done otherwise.

As this program developed, it became clear that learning about the Trailblazers could shed light not only on the possible future of publicly engaged governing, but also on the question of what spurs innovation in local government. Trailblazers' reflections, and ours, on this topic are included here, too.

PART ONE

Chapter 1

WHY PUBLICLY ENGAGED GOVERNING: THE EVOLUTION OF THE GOVERNMENT TRAILBLAZER PROGRAM

DISCONNECTS BETWEEN THE PUBLIC AND GOVERNMENT

When this program started in 2003, performance measures, when used at all by cities, counties and states, generally were developed by government managers without consulting the public, and, for the most part, performance reports were available for internal governmental use only.

We learned from focus group research that we conducted between 1995 and 2001 that the public and government use different ways to gauge government performance. The nature of the interactions with government employees and agencies is critical to the way people judge an agency and government itself.[3] However, governments rarely measure if the public finds their agency interactions responsive to their needs, respectful and accessible to all.

Governments may measure and report about, for example, how many tons of garbage were collected and how many people were assigned to this task, or how much asphalt was laid and how much it cost—important factors for workforce planning, purchasing and financial reporting. But the public cannot assess whether these numbers tell them if and where the streets are cleaner or the roadways are smooth as a result of these efforts. And it is outcomes such as these that the public cares about. We also learned that people would be interested in, using these

---

[3] See Cohn Berman, *Listening to the Public.*

examples, if the amounts purchased were sufficient—too much or too little—or at the best prices, and what quality and efficiency standards are being applied. Government too must care about, obtain and disseminate reliable information about these services and their outcomes because it is the job of government to deliver services and information that the public needs.

When workload, input, cost or personnel data are the only measures that government uses, government employees can lose sight of the purpose of their efforts. They can conclude that collecting a certain amount of garbage or laying "x" tons of asphalt is the work expected of them, regardless of how it is collected (spilling some on the sidewalk, collecting refuse later than scheduled, in the former example; on roads that are already smooth or are in some neighborhoods, avoiding others, in the second example).

Thus, a disconnect occurs when the public is excluded from the performance measurement, reporting and management activities. The result is misunderstandings between what the public needs and wants from its government and the way government decides to deliver and prioritize its work. Antipathy, distrust and accusations can follow. [Exhibit 1]

Exhibit 1: Disconnects Between Government and the Public

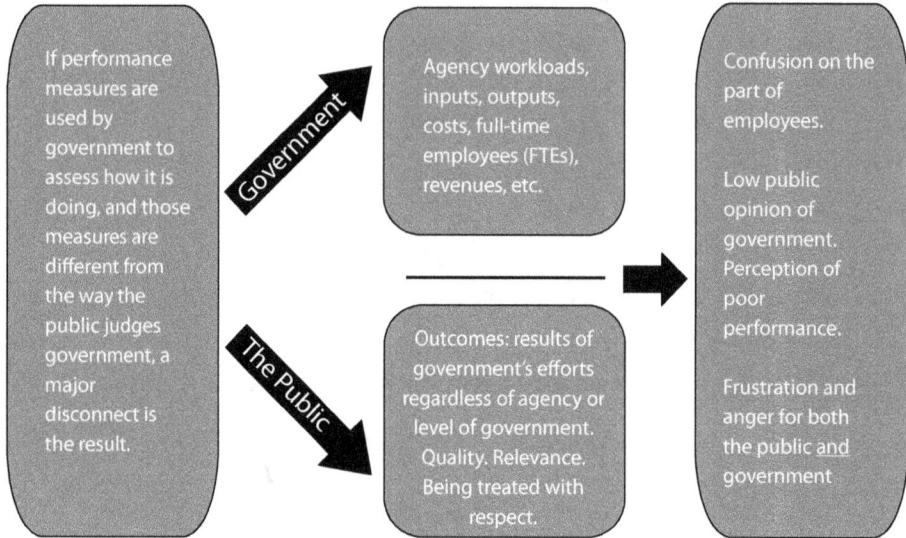

The Trailblazer Program has encouraged local and county governments to introduce new ways to learn from the public about information the public wants and needs from their government, communicate with the public, providing ongoing explanations and feedback about their suggestions and issues, and be responsive to the public on a continuing basis, thereby minimizing the disconnects previously mentioned.

HOW THE TRAILBLAZER PROGRAM EVOLVED

In 2003, the Center on Government Performance (CGP), with support from the Alfred P. Sloan Foundation[4], launched a Demonstration Grant Program to encourage local and state governments to test proposed criteria for reporting government performance[5], produce and disseminate to the public annual performance reports, and consider the public's feedback in preparing subsequent reports.

We announced this new program in major public administration publications, at local and national conferences of government representatives, in email distributions and by word of mouth by Governmental Accounting Standards Board (GASB) leaders and others.

Selection Criteria

Criteria for selecting the initial Trailblazers were recommended in consultation with the GASB and the Alfred P. Sloan Foundation. All prospective candidates, at a minimum, had to be collecting performance data. To be accepted into the program, candidates were required to have the head of the government endorse and support its participation and designate a person (the Trailblazer project director) to be responsible for starting, managing and reporting about their initiative.

An electronic application form available from our website was designed to ease the

---

[4] In 1995, the Alfred P. Sloan Foundation began a nationwide program, Making Municipal Governments More Responsive to Their Citizens, to "make citizen-informed and citizen-based government performance measurement and reporting widespread, normal and expected."

[5] In 2003, the Governmental Accounting Standards Board (GASB) issued *Reporting Performance Information: Suggested Criteria for Effective Communication* "to provide guidelines to state and local governments to enhance the production of external SEA [Service Efforts and Accomplishments] reports through use of sixteen suggested criteria. These criteria were developed by studying state and local governments currently using SEA measures and studying the work of other national and international organizations." The GASB interviewed the demonstration grantees and conducted extensive research before issuing, in 2010, the *Suggested Guidelines for Voluntary Reporting*. CGP distributed copies to all Trailblazers.

application process for applicants. A panel of government practitioners, academics and other experts in the field of government performance screened applications. Final decisions were made by CGP after further consultation with the Alfred P. Sloan Foundation and the GASB.

Obligations of Trailblazers

Trailblazers had to agree to:

- Make their existing performance measures and reports accessible to the public
- Find out from the public what information they would like from government and how they prefer the information to be presented in the future
- Take some or all of the public's requests into consideration in producing future performance measures and reports
- Test/try applying the GASB Suggested Criteria and report their experiences back to CGP and the GASB
- Share their experiences, solutions and challenges with other Trailblazer government representatives and CGP by:
    - Attending annual Trailblazer conferences
    - Participating in CGP's Trailblazer listserv
    - Submitting brief quarterly status reports to CGP

Of the initial 27 governments selected, three governments withdrew shortly after their acceptance into the program, one as a result of unanticipated leadership changes and concomitant lack of support, another as a result of their inadequate budget and personnel resources, and a third faced unanticipated conflicting time deadlines. Of the 24 remaining grantees, one government produced a performance report but was ultimately not able to disseminate it to the public, and another government asked for an extension to fulfill the grant requirements, which it eventually satisfied.

Expansion

The success of the demonstration program led CGP to expand the program's reach to more governments, including some in Canada. A new group of 23 Trailblazers joined the program in 2007. In 2009 and again in 2010, the program was expanded to include 11 and 12 additional governments, respectively.

As the program grew, we encouraged Trailblazers to go beyond the initial requirements by:

- Adapting market research methods to listen to the public about their views on their government's performance and performance measures
- Adapting technology to meet the objectives of the program—in the ways they reach out to and listen to the public and in the ways in which they disseminate information to the public
- Using publicly-informed performance measures to align existing and new government operations with the public's needs and desires, whenever possible

Incentives

Trailblazer governments were offered stipends to help support their Trailblazer initiative: $30,000 over a three-year period for the first group; $12,500 for the second 2007- 2008 grantees; $5,000 for the 2009 and 2010 groups. In addition, they attended expense-paid national meetings of Trailblazers to share experiences and learn from one another.

As of this writing, we have worked directly with 70 governments in the U.S. and Canada, providing them with: modest financial incentives, recognition for their role as innovators in government, collegial opportunities with rigorous agendas to meet with and otherwise communicate with one another to share accomplishments, challenges, advice and ways to communicate with us on an ongoing basis. Concurrently, we documented their work and the developments of this initiative, the findings of which appear in this report.

Chapter 2

WHO THE TRAILBLAZERS ARE—THE GOVERNMENTS AND THE PEOPLE

The 70 Trailblazer governments span the U.S. and Canada. Most are cities or counties; some are special governmental entities. Three statewide government organizations were part of the original demonstration grant group as was one Indian tribe. [Exhibits 2 and 3]

Exhibit 2: Where the 70 Trailblazer Governments Are

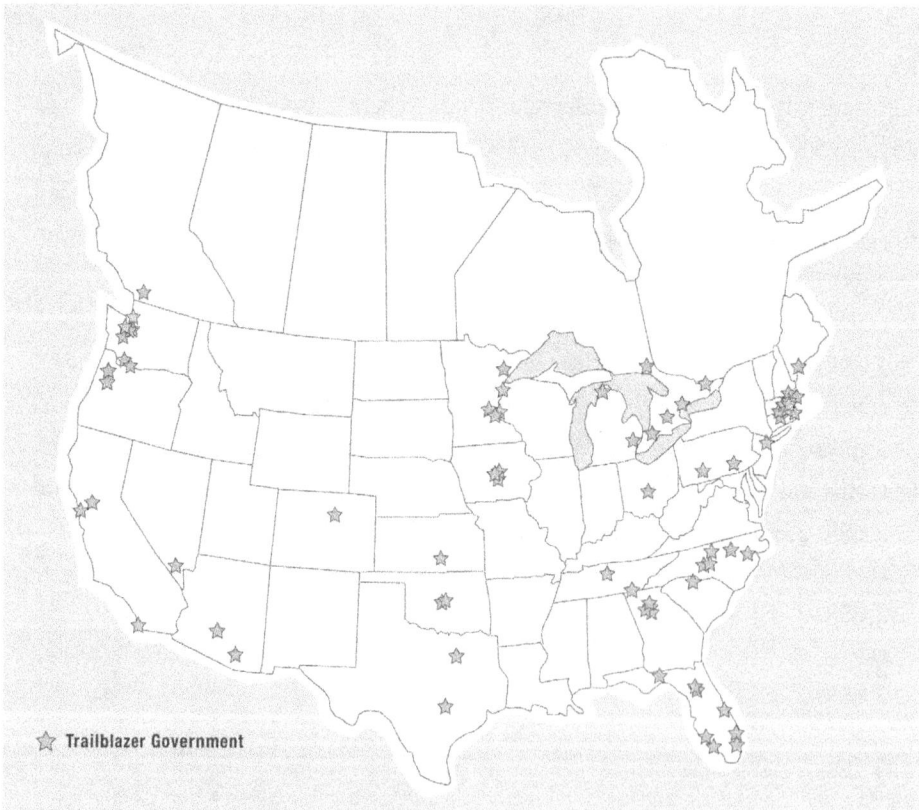

Source: Center on Government Performance

Exhibit 3: Trailblazer Governments, 2003-2010

	Type of Government	Population (in thousands)	Budget (in millions)	Year Started As Trailblazer
Alachua County, FL	County	240	$170	2009
Alcohol, Drug and Mental Health Services of Franklin County, Ohio	County Board	N/R	$6	2007
Alpharetta, GA	City	36	$44	2003
Amesbury, MA	City	18	$54	2009
Ankeny, IA	City	27	$32	2003
Atlanta Watershed Department, GA	City Agency	N/R	$532	2010
Austin, TX	City	681	$1,900	2003
Bellevue, WA	City	117	$587	2003
Brisbane, CA	City	3.5	$14	2010
Cambria County, PA	County	150	$140	2007
Chattanooga, TN	City	156	$215	2003
Collier County, FL	County	330	$530	2010
Columbia River Gorge Commission in Oregon and Washington	Commission	N/R	$1.77	2009
Cumberland County, PA	County	225	$185	2007
Decatur, GA	City	19	$16.9	2007
Denver (City and County), CO	City-County	580	$1,900	2007
Derby, KS	City	20.5	$25	2007
Des Moines, IA	City	199	$468	2003
Duluth, MN	City	84	$316	2009
Durham, NC	City	193	$260	2003
Eugene, OR	City	142	$159	2003
Gainesville, FL	City	125	$259	2010
Greater Sudbury, ON	City	160	$508	2007
Guilford County, NC	County	449	$521	2007
Iona McGregor Fire District, FL	Fire District	66	$18	2009
Iowa	State	2,900	$13,500	2003
Irving, TX	City	198	$183	2003
King County, WA	County	1,800	$3,890	2007

continued-

	Type of Government	Population (in thousands)	Budget (in millions)	Year Started As Trailblazer
Lauderhill, FL	City	57	$62	2003
Little Traverse Bay of Odawa Indians in Michigan	Nation Tribe	3.8	$20	2003
London, ON	City	356	$402	2007
Maple Ridge, BC	City	75	$100	2007
Maricopa County, AZ	County	3,100	$2,500	2003
Miami-Dade County, FL	County	2,300	$5,000	2003
Minneapolis, MN	City	383	$1,120	2003
Nashville and Davidson County (Metropolitan Government), TN	City-County	600	$1,500	2007
New Bedford, MA	City	100	$282	2009
Newark, NJ	City	263	$665	2007
Newport, RI	City	27	$110	2007
North Attleboro, MA	Town	29	$70	2010
North Las Vegas, NV	City	178	$516	2009
Oklahoma City, OK	City	550	$540	2010
Oklahoma Health Care Authority	State Authority	N/R	$2,700	2007
Oregon Progress Board*	State	3,500	N/R	2003
Ottawa, ON	City	889	$2,200	2007
Palm Bay, FL	City	100	$153	2007
Pitt County, NC	County	156	$206	2010
Rock Hill, SC	City	67	$164	2010
Saco, ME	City	17	$38	2003
Salisbury, NC	City	28	$53	2003
San Diego Unified Port District	Port District	N/R	$125	2003
Sandy Springs, GA	City	99	$97	2010
Snohomish County, WA	County	672	$591	2007
Solano County, CA	County	425	$982	2009
Somerville, MA	City	80	$164	2007
Springfield, MA	City	150	$531	2009
St. Louis County, MN	County	200	$317	2007

continued-

	Type of Government	Population (in thousands)	Budget (in millions)	Year Started As Trailblazer
Stanly County, NC	County	59	$59	2009
Tallahassee, FL	City	178	$133	2010
Toronto, ON	City	2,730	$9,800	2007
Tucson, AZ	City	487	$696	2003
University Place, WA	City	31	$20	2009
Vancouver, WA	City	155	$219	2007
Washington County, MN	County	211	$140	2003
Washington State Department of Social and Health, Children's Administration	State Agency	N/R	$907	2003
Waterloo (Region of), ON	County	515	$690	2007
Wayne County, MI	County	2,100	$2,250	2010
West Boylston, MA	Town	7.5	$20	2009
West Hartford, CT	Town	61	$69	2003
Woodbury, MN	City	59	$61	2009

Source: Budget and population figures were self-reported by Trailblazers at the time of their application to the program. Budget figures for Canadian governments are in Canadian dollars.
* The Oregon Progress Board was defunded in 2009.
N/R - Not Relevant.

Cities and towns. Thirty-nine of the Trailblazer governments are cities; three are towns. The largest, Toronto, Ontario, with a population of 2.7 million, had an operating budget of 9.8 billion CAD. The smallest Trailblazer city, in population and budget, is Brisbane, California, with 3,500 residents and an operating budget of $14 million. In addition to Toronto, four other Canadian governments participated: Greater Sudbury, London, Ottawa and Maple Ridge.

Counties. Sixteen counties joined the Trailblazer Program. Miami-Dade County, Florida, which encompasses 35 municipalities including Miami, Hialeah and Coral Gables plus unincorporated areas, has the largest budget, $5 billion, for its population of 2.3 million residents. Maricopa County, Arizona serves the largest population of the Trailblazer counties—3.1 million residents—with a $2.5 billion budget. At the other extreme, Stanly County, North Carolina has a population of 59,000 and operates with a $59 million budget. The Region of Waterloo in Canada is similar to a county government in the U.S., and is included in this category.

Two city-county governments, the City and County of Denver, Colorado and the Metropolitan Government of Nashville and Davidson Counties, Tennessee, serve populations of 580,000 and 600,000, respectively. Their corresponding budgets are $1.9 billion and $1.5 billion.

States. At the statewide level, the State of Iowa participated with the first group of Trailblazers as did the Oregon Progress Board, the Oklahoma Health Care Authority and Washington State Department of Social and Health Services, Children's Administration.

Special Entities. The Little Traverse Bay Bands of Odawa Indians; Columbia River Gorge Commission, in parts of the states of Oregon and Washington; San Diego Unified Port District; Alcohol, Drug and Mental Health Services of Franklin County, Ohio; Watershed Department of Atlanta, Georgia and the Iona McGregor Fire District, Florida participated in the Trailblazer Program as well.

Clusters. Exhibit 2 portrays what turned out to be some unexpected clustering of Trailblazers in certain geographical areas, notably in New England, Florida and the Northwest. After one government in the group joined the Trailblazer Program, others nearby followed. Regional benchmarking programs encouraged communications among their towns, cities and counties.

Another cluster of five governments in Ontario, Canada was expected. They are part of a long-established benchmarking initiative of governments in that province, the Ontario Municipal Benchmarking Initiative (OMBI). Their visionary director, executive committee and five of their members—four municipalities and one regional government—chose to join the Trailblazer Program to introduce public reporting of their group's performance measures and report and conduct focus group research to determine from members of the public how reports could be shaped to better inform them.

Where Trailblazer Project Directors Worked

In 2003, at the start of the program, most Trailblazer project directors were working in the budget and finance offices of their governments. [Exhibit 4] Indeed, performance data gathering and reporting was primarily a budget-related function and probably still remains so in many governments. They held positions such as Director of Finance, Finance Officer, Budget Director, Chief Financial Officer and Auditor. Three who worked in their budget office had titles that included the word "performance" as well.

It is relevant to note that, other than at budget hearings, finance and budget officers typically do not have occasions to interact with the public. They have few opportunities for informal discussions and the give and take that public engagement contemplates—a fact that challenged the success of the program from the outset.

By 2011, when the last Trailblazer group was selected, the dominant location where Trailblazers worked had changed considerably, with the preponderance of participants then working out of their executive offices. Only 26 percent were in the budget/finance/audit departments, compared to 37 percent eight years earlier. [Exhibits 4 and 5]

Exhibit 4: Departments Where 24 Trailblazer Directors Worked, 2003

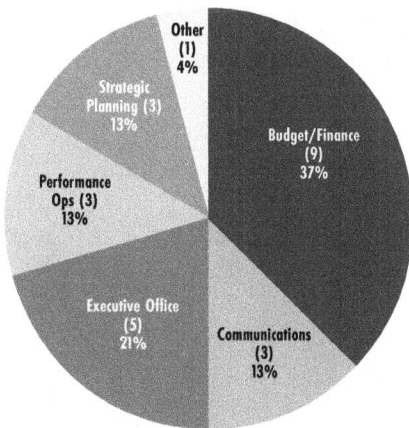

Source: Center on Government Performance, Trailblazer Applications

Exhibit 5: Departments Where 70 Trailblazer Directors Worked, 2011

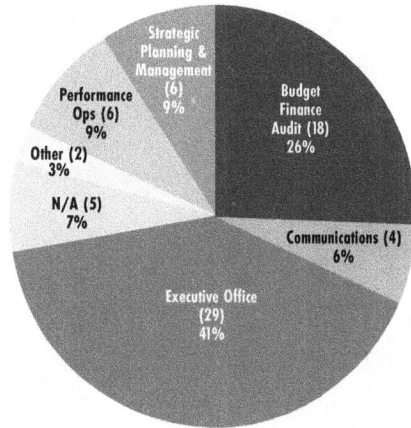

Source: Center on Government Performance, Trailblazer Reports

Trailblazers tell us that this shift reflects an increasing interest on the part of top city and county executives in opening new communication lines with the public, reaching out to neighborhoods not often consulted and making data about government performance available. It may also reflect the influence in the U.S. and Canada of the aforementioned "Making Municipal Governments More Responsive to Their Citizens" initiatives sponsored by the Alfred P. Sloan Foundation to "make citizen-informed and citizen-based government performance measurement and reporting widespread, normal and expected."

Although the level of interest in reaching out to the public rose to the top levels of local governments during the time of this study, those doing the day-to-day work—sometimes even introducing these initiatives—included people holding the title of "analyst." In fact, 21 percent of the 2011 Trailblazer project directors held that title, as contrasted with four percent in 2003. [Exhibits 6 and 7] Some analysts had recently completed Master's programs in public policy, public management, public administration or related disciplines and were eager to implement what they had learned during their studies.

As more emphasis has been put on performance measurement, reporting and management, "Performance" units positioned within executive offices have emerged along with new titles ranging from Performance Analyst through to Performance Manager.

Exhibit 6: Positions Held By 24 Trailblazer Directors, 2003

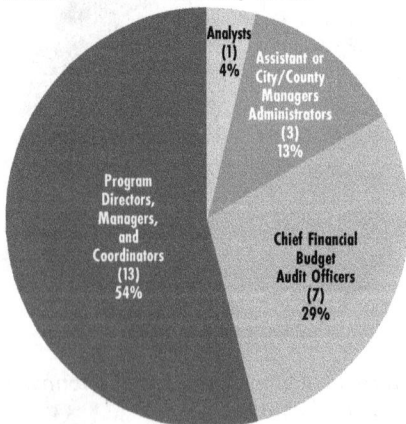

Analysts (1) 4%

Assistant or City/County Managers Administrators (3) 13%

Program Directors, Managers, and Coordinators (13) 54%

Chief Financial Budget Audit Officers (7) 29%

Source: Center on Government Performance, Trailblazer Applications

Exhibit 7: Positions Held By 70 Trailblazer Directors, 2011

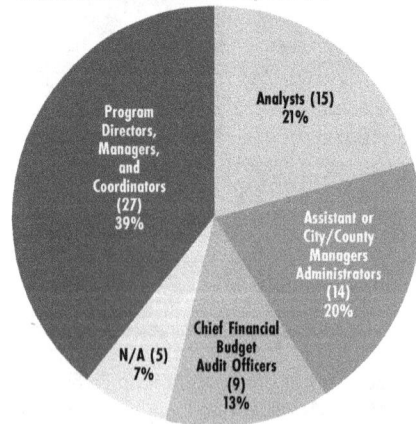

Program Directors, Managers, and Coordinators (27) 39%

Analysts (15) 21%

Assistant or City/County Managers Administrators (14) 20%

Chief Financial Budget Audit Officers (9) 13%

N/A (5) 7%

Source: Center on Government Performance, Trailblazer Reports

PART TWO

Chapter 3

AS TRAILBLAZERS BEGAN THEIR WORK

A prerequisite for becoming part of the Trailblazer Program was that a government already had in place the practice of collecting data about its operations. Frequently, the data were compiled and managed by the government's budget operation, and after scrutiny some or all information was included in its annual budget document—often a highly detailed technical volume or volumes not designed for the general public nor easily accessible to the general public.

Indeed, the annual budget document was the public place where the performance data often resided when most Trailblazers joined the program. Some budget documents were hundreds of pages in length containing seemingly endless pages of computer printouts and obscure technical terminology. Some governments produced separate annual reports or newsletters that informed the public about agency functions, major accomplishments, the names and pictures of agency heads and telephone numbers. Selected operations and performance data that government officials wished to feature, along with usually favorable results from a citizen satisfaction survey if one was conducted, were sometimes included.

For the most part, the reports were not designed for public consumption nor were they made available for the public's easy access. Even as government websites became ubiquitous, these documents were not featured. Considerable time and effort was required to locate them on the site. Some governments were members of benchmarking initiatives with other governments in their state or region or, on a national basis, with the International City/County Management Association (ICMA) in which they produced indicators using common definitions and methods. Their measures and reports were used for internal purposes only and were not available to the public.

Typically, governments had been collecting information about their:

- Costs for personnel, overtime, other than personnel expenses;
- Revenues;
- Major workloads such as number of requests made, number of applications filed;
- Outputs such as number of arrests, number of permits granted, number of miles of roadways paved, tons of asphalt laid, books purchased, etc.

They maintained data about their workforce, demographic information, facts about the area and other facts and figures that their local legislators requested. City- or county-wide crime rates and response times for emergency services were maintained, usually by the agencies involved.

Most significantly, if and when reports were prepared by governments before they entered the Trailblazer Program, they did not reflect the qualities of a publicly engaged government. See Exhibits 8 and 9.

- The content of the reports were decided upon by government alone.
- The design, style, format and frequency of the reports were decided upon by government alone.
- No mechanisms, procedures or opportunities were available for the government to receive feedback from the public about:
  - What information the public wanted,
  - How the public preferred the information to be presented,
  - Their thoughts about the existing report and the information in it.
- With perhaps one or two exceptions, the data and the reports were not disseminated to all members of the public.

Exhibit 8: Has the Public Been Involved in Formulating Your Performance Measures?

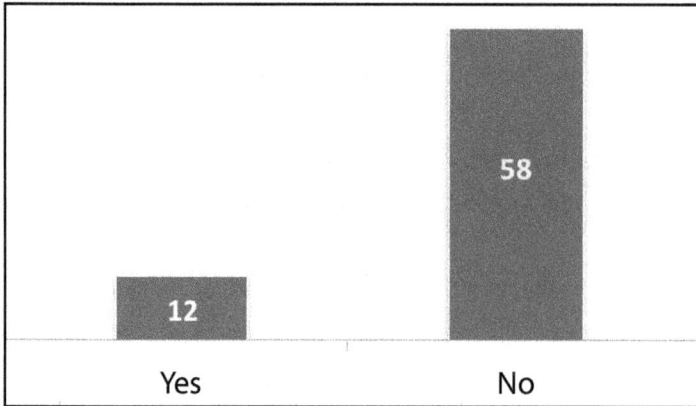

Source: Center on Government Performance, Trailblazer Applications. The governments that reported that they involved the public, consulted with previously appointed or pre-existing citizen boards or advisory committees whereas the Trailblazer Program emphasizes widespread outreach.

Exhibit 9: Has the Public Been Involved in Commenting on Your Performance Reports?

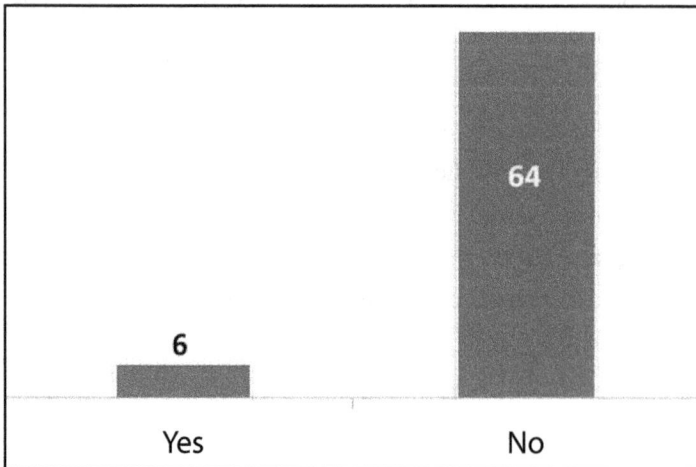

Source: Center on Government Performance, Trailblazer Applications. The governments that reported that they involved the public, consulted them primarily in the context of reviewing strategic plans whereas the Trailblazer Program emphasizes obtaining the public's views on the full range of government operations.

Chapter 4

CHALLENGES OF BEING A TRAILBLAZER

Trailblazers are charged with the task of introducing new concepts and practices into their governments. Anxiety and resistance are common reactions to change. Anticipating and understanding these reactions—from within the government and outside it—presented the first of many challenges for beginning Trailblazers and anyone introducing an innovation, despite the fact that they have the support of top management. Starting up is time consuming, involves learning new techniques, tests the project director's skills at working with reluctant colleagues, members of the public and elected and appointed officials they do not know and is fraught with trial and error and uncertainty.

In addition, other challenges involved:

- Working with limited and declining fiscal resources
- Having multiple assignments with insufficient time to manage all of them
- Learning about and deciding upon a methodology that will engage the public and enable government to learn about the public's views in a productive, non-confrontational manner
- Continuing the work while experiencing changes in elected and appointed officials
- Being sensitive to political concerns on the local and broader scene
- Reporting about bad news

Over the course of the Trailblazer Program, some challenges forced the suspension of the work. In one city, the person who championed this work left the government; his successor was less enthusiastic and the program faltered. Although the public had been consulted and a report prepared reflecting their views, in another city, the Mayor's office halted its release. Several years later, after a change in administration, the work resumed with renewed energy and support. And in a third situation, after severe revenue declines and resulting personnel cuts, one of the most enthusiastic cities ended their entire performance measurement program. Some other cities experienced less dramatic turns, but the work rose higher when the original supporter was on the scene.

Despite the myriad obstacles facing Trailblazers as they worked to start and then institute some aspects of publicly engaged governance, we can report that it took about one year for them to start up the program. By the end of the first year, most governments had heard from the public at least once and were then engaged in revising their performance measures or reports and were feeding back the information to the management teams and legislators who make policy or run operations.

Time and again, we observed that the support for this program and the skills and determination of the project director and head of government were central to its survival. Despite the common saying that "no one is indispensable," we found that some people truly are indispensable and should be acknowledged as such.

Examples of the way some Trailblazers described their challenges follow:

✓ **Starting Up**

> *"Just trying to decide where to start at this point, but this meeting/ networking opportunity [a Trailblazer national meeting] has given me plenty of ideas."* (County budget/finance/audit officer)

> *"The major challenges are getting the initial approval from all of the participating bodies, and collaborating and developing a shared and sustained consensus about how to proceed in a timely and coordinated fashion with several other projects in progress."* (Project director)

"I feel we are still crawling before we can walk and run with this initiative, but one of the initial successes is the awareness that has been brought to the forefront. Department heads, town boards and commissions and employees are much more cognizant of the concerns of the residents and acknowledge the work that lies ahead." (Project director)

✓ **Finding Time and Resources**

"The biggest challenge was finding the time to dedicate to the project because no one in the organization has a job that just focuses on performance measurement. The only way I overcame it was working overtime. I think this is a challenge that you will find in most small organizations, and it is important to find someone who is passionate about the issue." (City planning director)

"The intern provided assistance, but we have no ongoing resource." (County budget/finance/audit officer)

"One of my biggest challenges has been finding the time to work on and implement some of the recommendations made during our focus group process. .... The city's performance measurement program is one of my many duties. There are many great ideas and practices that I have learned of either through the Trailblazer meetings or via the focus groups, but I do not have the time or resources to implement them all. Therefore, I have concentrated on some of the key recommendations that have come out of this process, which has included developing a citizen focused report and occasional articles in our monthly newsletter." (City analyst)

✓ *Gaining Acceptance*

"The performance measurement and reporting effort faced a major hurdle of being accepted by department heads as something other than the next management 'flavor of the month' gimmick. By virtue of its being done for four years running, and now that it is likely going to be part of the leadership concerns, that hurdle may be overcome. As well, several departments have benefited from the information and so support the program for that reason." (City budget/finance/audit officer)

"Another challenge is keeping cabinet members and other managers engaged in the process.... We continue to explore ways to ensure that it is clear that PM is an ongoing process and not a one-time endeavor or something they have to address once a year for the budget book." (County budget/finance analyst)

"[There was] covert opposition in senior/executive leadership; outward verbal support but little action and follow thru. [We need a] cultural shift in the organization that still has an 'old-fashioned' foothold." (Program manager)

"One of the biggest ... was challenging the 'we've always done it this way' mentality. I found the easiest way to combat that was to show how citizen informed performance measurement helps meet the larger goals of the city, engages citizens, and really isn't that hard to do." (City planning director)

"Getting the bean counters in the finance department to understand it. We spend more on processing $5,000 than we do on results." (City planning director)

"While supportive of the concept of the grant, had a difficult time changing the report, especially reporting 'bad news' [but] did implement changes only if I wrote them and took responsibility for them." (City planning director)

"Some members of our legislature were resistant to the idea of a city office running neighborhood meetings. They argued that having constituent meetings was their function.... They eventually became enthusiastic supporters.... We worked hard to co-sponsor all meetings and to include them in the planning process for each ... meeting." (City program director)

✓ **Obtaining Accurate Data**

"The key challenge was developing a program that allowed for the collection of accurate, useable data without adding steps to existing workflow. Overcoming the issue in a cost-effective manner was the basis for our Trailblazer Grant project." (City executive)

"Establishing auditable measures and collecting the data is the most difficult aspect." (Finance officer)

✓ **Involving the Public**

"I believe I was able to overcome the methodology challenge by hiring a focus group specialist with the grant funding. I think we did a somewhat creative job by developing the mock scorecards to use as the basis for the discussion...." (County performance manager)

"The major challenge we faced was getting the public involved in a discussion about municipal performance measures and reporting..." (City executive)

"The biggest challenge has been to engage immigrant residents. We had four meetings with three different immigrant communities and had very

low attendance. We have not overcome this challenge. I believe it requires much more of a community organizing orientation than we have taken to date. We do have staff members who serve this function in the city, and for our [next] meetings with these groups, I will be working with these staff members to have them advise us and help with relationship building." (City program director)

✓ **Disseminating to the Public**

"The biggest challenge we have faced and continue to face is deciding the best, most effective manner of getting our performance reporting out to the public. This issue could be worsened due to recent budget cuts and constraints that our organization has faced." (County communications/ public affairs)

"A major challenge of the program has been learning to redevelop a large traditional integrated report to a series of smaller documents with a more individualized, directional focus." (County executive)

"One of the most important things in reaching myriad audiences with performance outcome information is tools to make the information have appeal to different readers. Some readers focus exclusively on charts and graphs, others extract data from narrative and still others are interested only in the actual human impact. Most want some combination of all of these." (State communications/public affairs)

✓ *Politics*

"The major challenges were not getting caught up in political issues. There were a lot of things going on during the time period.... In an extremely political environment, it is difficult to honestly discuss shortcomings. This was especially exacerbated by the political situation with the ... incumbents running for reelection." (County budget/finance/audit officer)

"Reporting on performance becomes a VERY political endeavor as it relates to elected officials." (City communications director)

"Only time will tell. Our plan has been to make performance measurement and reporting and public engagement such powerful and successful tools that any incoming administration will want to sustain and even build on this administration's commitment and success." (State project director)

Chapter 5

WHAT TRAILBLAZERS DID THAT WAS DIFFERENT

REACHING OUT—HOW THEY LISTENED TO THE PUBLIC

All Trailblazer governments were required to reach out to discover the public's views and recommendations about performance measures and reports. At our early meetings with each new group, the Center on Government Performance (CGP) provided presentations and demonstrations and facilitated discussions about the focus group research methodology we used and the findings that emerged. We provided Trailblazers with copies of our *Listening to the Public* book that covers the methodology in greater detail. We provided advice and encouragement to any Trailblazer who sought it as they started this new venture.

We encouraged, but did not require, Trailblazers to use focus group research as they reached out to the public. We did insist that the outreach include representative members of their public, from various neighborhoods, economic strata, ethnicities, ages, etc. And we strongly recommended that professional market researchers or facilitators be consulted to design the sessions with the public. Furthermore, we recommended that the sessions be conducted in a neutral setting rather than in a government office.

In every instance, this was a new approach to listening to the public for Trailblazers. For some, communicating directly with the public occurred rarely since many worked in budget operations rather than in delivering direct services. Initially then, this was a challenging undertaking for them and their governments. They expressed doubts about the public's interest in government and feared that no one would agree to attend a focus group session or respond to surveys. Few saw the advantage of consulting market researchers or facilitators and were confident that they could convene their own groups and elicit comments from them in their own offices. Some who were familiar with using citizen satisfaction surveys were confident that those surveys could serve the purpose without further re-design.

In 2008, we issued *TIPS for Conducting FOCUS GROUPS to Develop Government Performance Measures and Reports* and *TIPS for Conducting CITIZEN SURVEYS to Develop Government Performance Measures and Reports* (www.fcny.org/cgp). These were prepared to help guide Trailblazers and others as they assess the advantages, sequencing and usefulness of each of these methods.

There were some false starts. For example, one Trailblazer convened a session in the budget office, inviting people known to that office. Instead of fruitful conversation and new insights, it became rife with confrontations as government representatives reacted defensively; the meeting ended with hard feelings and no new insights for either side. Their next attempts were more successful, using a professional market research firm that did broader recruitment and worked with that government's Trailblazer project director to develop a discussion guide. The sessions were held in a non-governmental facility.

Although at first, the Trailblazers were skeptical about their ability to interest the public in this project and to recruit even a few people to participate, once they applied themselves to the effort and sought professional and collegial advice, their solutions were remarkable and successful.

Several Trailblazers undertook a variety of outreach efforts to connect with underserved or new residents. They attended meetings in their neighborhoods and recruited local residents or others of appropriate ages to help engage different generations, facilitate understanding and translate conversations and questionnaires.

As more Trailblazers started executing their outreach and devising methods that suited their environment and met our requirements, confidence increased as did experimentation. As shown in Exhibit 10, almost a third of Trailblazers reported using both focus group and survey methodology to hear from the public. In the province of Ontario, five governments held separate focus group sessions asking members of their public to redesign the governments' reports, making specific recommendations and edits during the sessions. Trailblazers reported on their differing initiatives, critiqued one another, offered advice and shared solutions and caveats at our annual meetings.

Exhibit 10: Methods Used by Trailblazers to Obtain Feedback from the Public

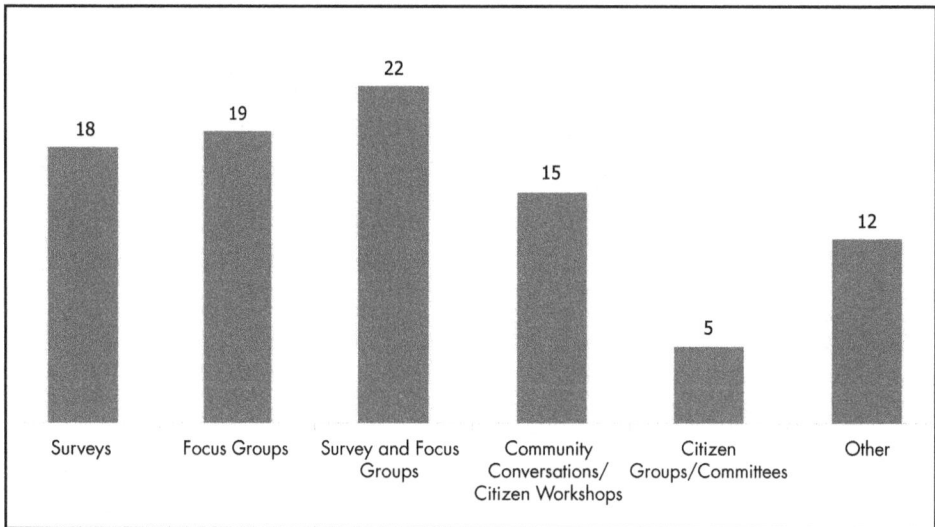

Source: Center on Government Performance, Trailblazer Reports

Governments also experimented with technology. For example, some conducted community meetings with well-planned scenarios, providing the public with "clickers" to register their responses that were recorded and tabulated immediately. This method allowed the facilitator and government representatives to explore the reasons for the responses during the session. Another government used what it called an "online collaboration tool," wherein they provided hosted "feedback forums," which allows residents to create, discuss and vote for ideas.

Some posted questions on their websites, had one-on-one interviews designed, inserted postcards with survey questions in government issued reports and tax bills and conducted online surveys. Other methods of feedback that governments used included customer surveys through a 311 system and customer service cards to help them understand how the public would like the agencies to improve.

Trailblazers described the value they placed on listening to the public:

> *"...The value of both citizen engagement and qualitative research has been demonstrated, and this has encouraged us to delve into further comparative citizen surveys/citizen engagement initiatives with our new skill sets to gain further insight and experience."* (Project manager)

> *"The Trailblazer Grant allowed more public input into the process; it has made our report less bureaucratic and more accessible to the average citizen."* (City project director)

> *"I believe [the city] has gained an ability to hear the voice of the citizen, and not just the city hall regulars and 'squeaky wheels' that typically dominate the conversation, but to feel like there is access to a majority opinion that helps guide how to make decisions."* (City budget/finance/audit officer)

> *"We have been able to refer to the public's desire for information in a tangible way by referring to our workshop feedback, providing a solid foundation for our requests for additional resources."* (City executive)

WHAT THEY HEARD

Shortly after the Trailblazers began listening to the public in these new ways, they reported back two types of observations that were surprising to them. One observation concerned the public's attitudes towards their local government, including views from people they normally do not hear from; the other reflected the views of public officials after hearing from the public at these sessions.

> **Initial Observation 1. Trailblazers learned that the public is interested in what their government is doing, cares about their government, wants information about government's performance and likes being involved in these consultative processes.**

"Our citizens have been responsive to the process and have thought that it is great that the city sought to do such reporting. The responses from the citizens have been extremely supportive in nature." (City project director)

"Our public is, for the most part, silent. Focus groups changed this phenomenon from silence to 'vocality'." (City budget/finance analyst)

"Reaffirmed to me that 'Average Joes' do in fact care about performance at the county. Will delete/add/modify many of the measures we are presenting. Citizens were 'delighted' that we were doing this work (performance reporting)." (County performance manager)

> **Initial Observation 2. Trailblazer governments discovered that some of the assumptions they have been making about what people need and want are incorrect.**

"Things we thought were clear weren't, measures we thought were meaningful weren't and there were gaps in information that we wouldn't have thought of without that input." (City performance manager)

"If you listen to the citizens, they will give you enormous feedback as to whether your data are even measuring what you need to be measuring. From feedback from the focus groups, we have reexamined data and found some to be lacking. We also found that we did not offer, in many cases, the data in which the citizens were most interested. Performance reports can be produced without involving the citizens, but involving them greatly improves the reliability and relevance of the quality of information." (County budget/finance/audit officer)

"We had citizens involved in the ... ratings and in reviewing the year one report and helping us design the workbooks and measures for year two. It definitely helped because the citizens had different priorities than staff as to what was important to measure." (City budget/finance/audit officer)

"We have learned that they are interested in the information we provide, but their questions on our report's content helped us to think differently about how we put the information out to them." (County program director)

"It was also clear from comments by the public and the community advisory group that their values and perceptions of 'what is important' did not always coincide with [ours]. A valuable lesson was learned in listening to disparate opinions and acknowledging their merit. [We need] to reinforce this behavior repeatedly in order to internalize the concept of partnership with those we serve." (Project director)

> Government reports were overwhelming in length, contained information of questionable interest to the general public and were not designed to be read by the public.

"The responses and comments we have received are that they are grateful for financial information and performance reporting that is easily readable, understandable and not overwhelming and intimidating." (Finance officer)

"Our report is too overwhelming for most readers." (City project manager)

"They specifically noted the need to simplify information that is presented to the public. They indicated that citizens would likely feel overwhelmed by the vast amount of information agencies include in their performance reports, so it is best to provide very basic information and the ability to drill down to more detailed information if they so choose." (Project director)

"Providing a comprehensive data set is overwhelming to most." (City budget/finance/audit officer)

> People want information that is relevant to them and that they can understand. They would like information summarized with further detail available for them to review as needed.
> They want current information about the outcomes of government efforts, by subject matter instead of by departmental jurisdiction.
> They want factual information ("without spin").
> And all the news, not just good news.
> Explanations and context.

"Citizens wanted more relevant measures [not just financial information]." (Finance officer)

"The most important lesson overall is that there is currently insufficient context in the measures." (County budget/finance/audit officer)

"We heard: Keep it simple and focused on the issues and outcomes the public cares most about. Don't hesitate to report bad news; it lends greater credibility to the entire report." (City performance manager)

"A few central themes surfaced that included: (1) keeping the reports short and making data easy to interpret; (2) tailoring reports to a specific service rather than lumping every service together in a single report; and (3) sending some reports on a more frequent basis to keep the data current." (City analyst)

"In our focus groups, the average citizens and the non-profit / community / neighborhood leaders say 'less is more' and 'make it pleasing to read / pleasing to the eye'." (City budget/finance analyst)

"People are very busy … We found that citizens want summary and then may ask for more detail. As long as we tell them how to find the detail we seem to be ok." (City performance manager)

"We heard clearly from the focus groups that they really liked a short… scorecard with links or direction to further information on the web… accessible, short performance reports with greater detail available on the Internet." (County performance manager)

"People … want … information in a user-friendly format." (City budget manager)

"… focus groups told us that they didn't care that the governance structure means that city government is not responsible for libraries, schools and parks. They still wanted performance data." (City program director)

"[We] did receive feedback that citizens liked the current performance report format; but they also wanted to see a scaled back version. The

rationale behind this is citizens only want to know high-level information when it comes to overall government performance. When it comes to a specific department they are interested in, they would like the opportunity to review a document with substance. I think this approach would be most effective in building citizen interest in [our] performance." (City performance analyst)

"We are learning that we need to simplify the presentation of complex information and angle it to address the issues or concerns of the citizens in any given year." (City executive)

"The biggest change is that we're thinking ... from the perspective of neighborhoods or special populations." (City program director)

People suggested practical and reasonable ways to improve the presentation of data.

"We found out that they are more interested in graphs and charts and simple language." (City executive)

"They also gave us ideas about formatting, such as including a map of our jurisdiction and a table of contents, and both these ideas were incorporated. There is no doubt their input improved the report both in scope of the information presented and in making it more readable for stakeholders." (Program manager)

"Recommendations included having a cleaner, more organized website with not too much copy on each page." (County communications/public affairs)

"I learned that there are some things that people would like changed in the report and that they would like more pictures throughout. I learned that some of the things that I found were important in some cases were not as important." (City project director)

HOW TRAILBLAZERS RESPONDED TO WHAT THEY HEARD FROM THE PUBLIC: CHANGING THEIR MEASURES AND REPORTS AND MAKING THEM MORE ACCESSIBLE

We did not require uniform responses by the Trailblazer governments to the public's suggestions and requests, respecting their different environments. The governments did, however, agree to take the public's reactions into account as they produced subsequent reports. Their responses were varied, imaginative, carefully considered and often influenced and were influenced by other Trailblazers' experiences. One example: the Assistant City Manager of a major midwest city strove to make their new performance report appealing to the public. He enlisted the city's artists to illustrate the report with their original works, giving them new audiences and delivering colorful, artwork to the public. The reports, which also contained clear presentations of data with contexts, explanations and good and not-so-good news were greeted with enthusiasm and interest each year, spanning a change in administration after an election. The response was so favorable that the City Manager decided to make copies available for every household in the city. Another Trailblazer city took heed and invited school children to illustrate that city's new performance report.

Responses by other Trailblazers, in their own words, follow.

✓ **Adopted the Public's Measures**

"We ultimately changed the measures we reported on the final scorecard based on the interests and needs we heard from the focus groups. The

feedback from the focus groups also allowed us to have some 'resiliency' when staff suggested an alternative or different measure; we were able to say 'the public really wanted to hear about this'." (County performance manager)

"Based on our grant experience, the report we publish next month will contain those measures that citizens identified as meaningful to their understanding of the program performance of our most critical programs." (Town executive)

"The new measurements are much more attuned to what would be meaningful to the public. We need to continue to improve these measures. We have also made the website more user-friendly. Finally, we put out a hard copy accountability report which should include the measurements next year." (County budget/finance/audit officer)

"As a result of citizen feedback to our initiative ... there will be a more effective performance measurement system. There will be an overhaul of performance measures as the new budget process begins. Some of the measurements will serve management; others will focus on the kinds of data our citizens have requested." (City budget/finance analyst)

"The content of [our] performance report has changed due to information received from respondents of the telephone survey and participants of the focus groups. It was apparent that measures which may be calculated in some departments are not useful to the citizens. It was important to see measures directly associated with Public Safety, Public Health and Social Services and Financial Service areas. Therefore, the scorecard shows these measures. The appearance of the report has changed dramatically. Charts and graphs help to draw a picture for our citizens making it easier to understand. The report is also four pages compared to our original 110-page report." (County budget/finance/audit officer)

"County officials are taking a closer look at performance data and how it affects the future for the citizens. Shifting to a citizen-centered standpoint. Perspective on the content and message will be from the citizen viewpoint, not agency viewpoint." (County executive)

✓ **Produced a Public Performance Report for the First Time**

"… [We] for the first time solicited citizen input in developing citizen-centric performance measures and produced the first ever report specifically devoted to performance reporting to the … constituents. The report requests continuous feedback from the public on improving the report format and contents." (County performance manager)

"We will produce a first ever citizen informed scorecard." (County performance manager)

"In the past, performance information was contained (buried) in the operating budget that might be 500 – 800 pages long. Also, in the past the budget document was not user-friendly. It did not contain information of program accomplishments and challenges. Improvements are now being made to the budget document and those will be influenced to some extent by the [new, separate] Report to Citizens." (City budget/finance/audit officer)

"We annually report on departmental performance measures in our budget document. We have begun to annually report on key community-wide measures in a report card that is distributed to the entire community." (City budget manager)

"[The City] will begin distributing an annual citizen report by the end of the first quarter for the previous year. This will be a high-level summary report that will indicate where a person interested in more detail can go

for further information. We hope to have the summary printed in the [newspaper], but that may be cost-prohibitive. We will provide more information on the Performance Initiative page of the City's website." (City budget/finance analyst)

"With the Trailblazer grant, the County, for the first time, produced a comprehensive report that included all the departments." (County budget/finance/audit officer)

✓ **Reports Are User-Friendly**

"A major significant change in [our] approach to performance is its attention to the audience. Sometimes, when governments are producing documents for its citizens, they forget who the audience is. The Trailblazer grant has expanded [our] approach to citizen documents. We are now focusing on how to simplify rather than using excessive jargon. In the long run, [we] understand that this is key in obtaining citizen involvement in [our] performance." (City performance analyst)

"The annual report was changed in response to citizen feedback by grouping measurements under themes instead of department areas and provided more contextual information." (City planning director)

"A major shift has been to move away from CAFR [Comprehensive Annual Financial Report] type reports." (County executive)

"The current report has been changed to make it more 'citizen-friendly' in content and format. Plans for the release of this year's document include instruction about where to go for more information and a limited online capability to drill down to access information with respect to specific services." (Project manager)

"We did totally revamp the annual report as a result of the focus groups."
(City planning director)

"The current practice has been modified to incorporate citizen feedback about existing measures and creation of new measures for every department. Citizen feedback is collected via focus groups and surveys."
(City planning director)

"The feedback complimented the [new] use of charts and graphs and the accompanying narratives that provided background and explained the 'why' behind data." (State project director)

"As a result of focus group input the decision to publish seven companion brochures was strongly reinforced. The separate brochures will be very useful to take to various meetings where the interest is geared toward a specific area such as smart growth or safe and healthy communities. It is felt that the separate brochures will also be more helpful to the public when searching the website for specific information." (County executive)

"The report is shorter, more graphs than charts, better organized and easier to read."
(City executive)

✓ **Disseminated to the Public, Using a Variety of Communication Methods**

"Citizens receive the community report card through the newspaper and have access to the other documents on the Internet or at the public library. However, our report card was developed with the participation of over 300 citizens, each assigned to one of eight committees (to line up with the eight citywide goals)." (City budget/finance/audit officer)

"We have a variety of different mechanisms for reporting information to internal and external audiences. A website for staff is available which allows employees to track performance outcomes.... We have periodic reports of special findings.... We report information annually through our ... annual performance report. In addition, twice a year we publish a report card aimed at citizens." (State communications/public affairs)

"A brochure that summarizes performance-related information was distributed publicly and to elected officials, and throughout county administration; the brochure also tells readers where to find additional performance information." (County executive)

"We have taken a major step toward providing a new level of data to our residents. This goes beyond the standard reporting that has been done through budgets and other typical documents, and provides a greater level of transparency. Prior to the grant award, the information was not provided to the public in a formal manner but was accessible if requested by the public. The grant award provided us the ability to develop a way to disseminate the information to the public through the Internet .... The website site offers citizens with the real-time ability to follow specific performance areas and to provide feedback." (City analyst)

"... we now have one report geared toward staff use (though it is available to the public), one directed toward the City Council and their strategic initiatives that is also intended to be very useful for our citizens, and a third report that is being developed specifically for our citizens that will be mailed to them. The contents and measures chosen for the citizen report have been selected based off of the feedback the city received from the focus groups we conducted with the Trailblazer grant." (City analyst)

"Probably the most dramatic change we made was putting more detailed performance data on the web and giving users the ability to drill down and more easily navigate the performance information." (County executive)

✓ **Provided Summary and Detailed Information**

"Created scorecards with neighborhood specific data in addition to annual report."
(City program director)

*"We learned that summary is more important to them than detail
(although they would like to know where to get the detail), and we learned
how best to communicate with them."* (City performance manager)

*"The current practice is to get away from long paper reports and have a
four-page performance scorecard and a more in-depth performance website.
This has been a gradual change but was enhanced by the grant and focus
group process."* (County performance manager)

*"We will be implementing a software application that will be an online
visual tool available to the public, council and staff. This interactive online
tool will be available on our website and will give users the option to learn
a little or a lot, depending on how far the user elects to drill down on the
interested subject. The characteristics of (1) availability upon user demand,
and (2) level of detail according to user preference were two of the key
messages we received from the public at our public workshop held earlier
this year (supported by our Trailblazer Grant)."* (City executive)

✓ **Their Government Enacted New Legislation Requiring
Performance Reporting to the Public**

*"[We] are focused more on citizen involvement than ever before.... We as a
city have recently updated our city charter through vote of referendum. By
law, we must now involve our citizens to a higher degree."* (City budget/
finance analyst)

"[The County's] legislation … now requires that 'No less than annually, the county manager shall prepare and make available to the public a performance report to the community. The report shall include, at a minimum performance data relative to goals and priority outcomes established in the County strategic plan.' The County now has a process in place to update the report annually." (County executive)

INFLUENCING POLICY AND MANAGEMENT PRACTICES

As Trailblazer work advanced, it became clear that government managers can and need to use the new publicly-informed outcome measures to clarify, design and improve policies and programs to better align the public's needs with governmental operations.

Recurring themes from all our focus group research are that people judge government by their first encounters, first impressions and interactions with government employees, with government websites and forms and processes. People want to be treated with respect and courtesy, in an even-handed, timely and responsive manner. They expect forms and procedures to be accessible and clear. They expect government facilities to be clean and display helpful signs. In response, some Trailblazers have developed ways to learn about and measure the public's satisfaction with their services and then feedback the information to their program staff on a continuing basis so that operations can be informed and revised accordingly to meet the public's needs. They have developed information and guidelines, surveys and focus groups to obtain information about their "customer" satisfaction and use it to make improvements in their services.

Below are reports from Trailblazers about how they are using public feedback in new ways to change the way they conduct the government's business.

✓ **Department Heads and Managers Use the Data to Evaluate Programs and Make Decisions**

"Departmental staff is now delving deeper into the data being collected and asking the all-important question 'why' when performance standards do not appear to be met. The performance data are, in those departments that are fully integrated into the initiative, now viewed in much the same way that a physician would view a symptom: as an indication of the real issue and the beginning of a line of questioning that will lead to a real solution." (City executive)

"Performance measures are used to make budget decisions, assess program operations and serve as an early warning mechanism to potential service delivery challenges. Some departments use measures to make hiring decisions...." (City performance manager)

"We are learning to ask department managers better questions to get to those key measures—such as what data do they need and use to make decisions and to evaluate whether or not the programs they manage are successful." (County budget/finance analyst)

"In the past, measures have been used when needed for justifications, but there has never been an emphasis on using performance measures to manage. With a new city manager, we are seeing a greater emphasis on using measures to manage....The new city manager ... continuously emphasizes performance measures, benchmarking and outcomes ... and wants to report the information/performance/progress." (City project manager)

"I would say that there is ample evidence that performance information and discussions about outcomes that programs and dollars achieve are part of meetings and decision-making venues in a way they had previously not

been. This is a change we can document during these past two to three years." (County analyst)

"The City's strategic alignment process supports this effort. This alignment now includes performance measurement. Our performance measurement report very nicely graphically depicts this alignment. This effort is being supported by all of management including the city administrator." (City budget/finance/audit officer)

"Beginning this year, departments have been holding 'performance review' sessions monthly; that is, senior management from each department meets once per month to formally review performance measures and discuss initiatives that may improve performance. Quarterly performance reviews are held by the Assistant County Managers with multiple departments of a strategic area (e.g. all of the public safety departments, all recreation and culture, etc.)." (County executive)

"Performance reporting data and considerations are 'at the table' with budgetary information and other considerations during the decision-making process. Commissioners request performance information and department heads and managers want to include it in their reports and routine conversations. We all have seen the public's interest in this information and positive reaction towards its accessibility in print and electronic methods." (County analyst)

✓ **Elected Officials Rely on the Data When Making Funding and Other Decisions**

"Elected officials use the language of our program when talking and they use the outcomes as a filter for decision making." (City program director)

"The citywide satisfaction survey is used more than any other performance measure. For example it has consistently shown high dissatisfaction with street conditions and the city government's effort to communicate with the public. Therefore, the council approved a large increase in funding for street resurfacing (tripling the number of lane miles recovered each year) and funded a citywide newsletter that is mailed to every household in [the city] on a quarterly basis." (City executive)

"Additionally, performance measures are now a required element of our business planning process, where funding deliberations are carried out by council in public meetings. This change came about as a result of the increased importance [our] administration department is placing on performance measures, partially due to the Trailblazer Program and the need to consider the measures during decision-making." (City executive)

"The first significant change ... is the application of performance data to the budget process. Resources are allocated based upon where they can offer the greatest return on investment or where they are needed to address specific issues. Prior to the introduction of the initiative, many such decisions were made based upon assumptions rather than quantified data." (City executive)

✓ **Improving Performance**

"I think that some services have improved as a result of this effort.... But I think the real change has been in how staff thinks about programs and services—what does it cost? What do the citizens get? Can costs be reduced without affecting service delivery? Especially in terms of budget crises, many department heads and senior management seem much more inclined to rely less on standard operating procedure (it is how we have always

done it) to think more analytically about what they do." (City budget/ finance/audit officer)

"With the performance data we have been able to gather, the central departments can make much better decisions about service delivery. An example of one department that improved management of programs and service delivery was the Transportation Department. This department is a smaller department, which had not used performance measurement much in the past. Using performance information, it improved customer service, on-time arrivals, and other performance measures greatly during the year." (County budget/finance/audit officer)

"Slowly the managers are taking ownership of the data and are reacting, in a positive way, i.e. by looking for ways to improve. Public awareness of the data is encouraging them to question management and public officials about what they do to improve service delivery." (City performance manager)

PART THREE

Chapter 6

TRAILBLAZERS AND INNOVATION

"Innovation is nothing more than finding, testing and exploiting
creative ideas to solve problems and achieve better value for citizens."
("Innovation, Risk and Control" CCAF~FCVI, Inc. Ottawa, 2010, p.2)

During annual Trailblazer meetings, we asked participants questions to elicit their reasons for joining the Trailblazer Program. We asked:

Why did your government apply for the Trailblazer Program?
Why did you and your government want to be Trailblazers?
How did you come to be in the role of initiating or sustaining this Trailblazer Program?

Initially, we wanted to gain insight from these responses to help us target new Trailblazers as the program expanded. As the program continued, we observed that Trailblazers shared enthusiasm for introducing the new approaches that the Trailblazer Program required, be it new ways to reach out to the public, new ways of listening to the public, new approaches to measuring performance, new ways to communicate the information to various audiences in written form and/or new ways to use the measures to improve performance.

Trailblazers appeared to enjoy the challenges of coming up with creative ways to implement the new program. They took pride in seeing the fruits of their efforts manifested in such ways as data being used by legislators to make decisions and useful new measures being developed while those not needed were eliminated. In short, Trailblazers were introducing innovations into their governments and liked doing it. Insight into the incentives and conditions that enabled innovation in this program can shed light on how and when innovation in the public sector begins and is sustained. With this ancillary benefit in mind, we present here some of the key elements that seem to account for the Trailblazers successes with their innovations.

Leadership. A requirement for entry into the Trailblazer Program was that the head of the government—be it a mayor, county executive, city manager, town executive, director of a commission or other public entity—endorse the application affirming approval and support of the project and, in the same application, the head of the government was required to name the person who would lead the program's day-to-day operations.

This requirement was inserted because it is common knowledge that any initiative in an organization is likely to be successful if "the boss" supports it. Therefore, we wanted to select among applicants where that support was present and success was probable.

In some places, the head of the government was fully engaged in the Trailblazer Program throughout its implementation. In others, the top leadership role was more distant, providing initial support and then handing the work over to the designated project director who had to assume the leadership role if the program were to succeed. In fact, it was not always the head of the government who initiated this program at all. As can be seen in Exhibit 11, although some Trailblazers reported that they undertook this initiative because "somebody above me asked me to do it," more Trailblazers reported that "I wanted to do this and suggested to my government that we do so."

> *"Wrote grant and took on responsibilities of program."* (City director)

> *"[It was] my initiative and grudging approval of the city manager."* (City budget/finance/audit officer)

> *"Through my own research, I thought it would be a good idea and*

•

suggested it to the county manager. He agreed but only if I would be responsible for implementation." (County budget/finance/audit officer)

"I personally support the intent." (County performance manager)

"I have been on the starting block with [our] performance initiative." (County analyst)

"I have taken this project on as a personal interest." (Town executive)

"I'm the primary individual responsible for performance management." (City executive)

It is of interest to note that some of the project managers were relatively new to government and brought the idea of citizen-informed performance measurement, reporting and management with them from graduate classes or professional conferences they had attended.

Moreover, there were changes in leadership at the top of some Trailblazer governments during the course of this program's operation and in those situations, it was up to the project manager to enlist the support of the new executive and keep the project advancing.

Exhibit 11: Reasons Trailblazers Gave in Response to the Following Questions:
Why did your government apply for the Trailblazer Program? Why did you and your government want to be Trailblazers? How did you come to be in the role of initiating or sustaining this Trailblazer Program?

Reasons for Becoming a Trailblazer (some respondents gave multiple reasons)	#
Provides opportunity to include/involve/reach out to the public	23
Will enhance our current performance measures, reports and/or methods	16
I wanted to do this and suggested to my government that we do so	16
People above me asked me to do it	11
Trailblazer Program provided funding	9
Will enable us to build networks with other governments	8
Interest was sparked by an outside organization or individual	8
Will give us the opportunity to make performance information accessible to the public	5
Wanted to be associated with this prestigious program; will help leave a legacy of accountability, transparency and performance improvement. Will help maintain our leadership in the field.	4
Will help my government move toward a culture of performance management	3

Source: Center on Government Performance, Trailblazers' Participant Surveys.

Changing the system. Making changes in the way their government operates was often mentioned during the Trailblazer meetings as a reason that impelled Trailblazers to join the program.

> *"After working our performance measures for 20+ years, I realized we were not reporting information which decisions could be made on. I decided we needed to change the style of measures we produce."* (City director)

> *"I have been collecting and compiling performance measures for five years now and have a great desire to move towards performance management."* (County budget/finance/audit officer)

"The [local university] emailed my boss. I am in charge of performance management and when my boss forwarded the Trailblazer information to me, I asked if we could participate because public engagement is missing from our current process." (City budget/finance analyst)

"I was personally not satisfied with our government's reporting of information to our citizens. At the time our [comprehensive annual financial report] CAFR was the major publication for external use. ... I wanted to take our effort to a higher level and the Citizen Engagement Project did that for us." (City performance manager)

"[The City] is trying to be a leader, to innovate and make government more transparent and effective." (City executive)

"Want to find ways to provide better customer service and to learn methods to better communicate with our county residents so that we can better meet their needs." (County executive)

"[We have operated] an internal management tool since its launch in 2004. However, we have always aspired to bring [that] data down to the resident level to solicit their feedback on priorities." (City program director)

"To further our efforts to develop a culture of performance management and citizen involvement." (County executive)

"... We wanted to improve our reporting. It was needlessly complex and completely inaccessible." (City performance manager)

Opportunity. As detailed immediately above, Trailblazers had a pre-existing desire to change the way in which they were operating their performance measurement and reporting systems, but they hadn't done so. They needed an opportunity. Joining the Government Trailblazer Program provided the opportunity to the interested governments by delivering funding, moral support, colleagues, deadlines, technical assistance and other incentives.

<u>Key staff willing or eager to take on the initiative.</u> In most governments, with the exception of very small ones with few in staff, a willing, able, enthusiastic staff member was essential to start the Trailblazer initiative and then operate it on a day-to-day basis, dealing with the inevitable setbacks and challenges involved in introducing change. This was a requirement of the Trailblazer Program, and indeed those managers are the Trailblazers managing the changes in their governments' operations.

***

As reported in this chapter, the circumstances surrounding the Trailblazers contained key elements that favor a climate conducive to innovation: leadership support, desire to change the system, an attractive opportunity provided by the Center on Government Performance of the National Center for Civic Innovation and the willingness by key, committed staff to undertake the day-to-day management of the initiative.

Chapter 7

ADVICE: COLLECTIVE WISDOM FROM THE TRAILBLAZER PROGRAM

"Good information makes good management. We should generate data in order to operate better and make better decisions and then report that data to the public. We should not just generate data simply for a public report with no internal use." (City executive)

At Trailblazer meetings and in questionnaires, we asked Trailblazers to share their advice with others who are mounting a public engagement initiative. At the annual Trailblazer meetings, we made presentations that addressed methodological matters and identified problems we observed in an effort to head off others making similar missteps. We also shared successes we observed. We described our experiences in targeting focus group discussions to elicit the reasons for ratings that emerged from previously-conducted large scale satisfaction survey. We compiled frequently asked questions that were posed to us as well as conundrums. The collective wisdom that emerged is summarized below.

Resistance

1. Expect resistance.
   - Be patient and keep in mind that change does not happen overnight.
   - But, be persistent. Do not give up!
   - Lay low when necessary, but do not give up!
   - Enlist support from the top, middle and bottom up. Figure out the best way to do this.
   - Be sure the staff knows what you are doing and why.

- Incorporate public engagement into job descriptions and individual performance evaluations.
- Share public engagement efforts from other localities with those in your government.

Performance Measures

2. Do spring cleaning of your performance measures.
   - Review what you have. Where are the gaps?
   - Are they being used? By whom? For what?
   - Are they needed?
   - Are they duplicative?
   - Can they be improved?
   - Can any be discarded?

3. Add and use:
   - Outcome measures.
   - Quality measures.
   - Measures of public satisfaction with your services and the reasons for their satisfaction or lack of satisfaction.

4. Data integrity is fundamental to the process. What can you do to assure accurate data collection and reporting?

Focus Groups[6]

5. Know your intent before starting a focus group project.

6. Hire nonpolitical, experienced professional market researchers who can help you:

---

[6] See *TIPS for Conducting FOCUS GROUPS to Develop Government Performance Measures and Reports*, National Center for Civic Innovation, 2008, www.fcny.org/cgp.

- Recruit a wide swath of people from various neighborhoods, major occupational, economic, generational, political and ethnic groups in your location.
- Create protocols for conducting focus groups.
- Identify appropriate facilitators to conduct the focus groups.
- Identify appropriate neutral facilities for conducting the focus groups.
- Elicit the public's views regarding their preferred way in which they would like to receive regular performance reports, their needs and expectations about the content and style of the report, its frequency and preferred dissemination modes.

7. Go to non-traditional sites to reach diverse communities, such as churches, community centers and other neighborhood places.

8. Be sure your focus groups are not made up of just the "usual suspects."

9. Do not conduct focus groups yourself or have them conducted in your offices. Use neutral space, preferably with an observation room and video and voice recording. Local universities have helped some Trailblazers.

10. Provide modest incentives to encourage people to attend the groups (e.g. gas cards to cover transportation expenses).

Surveys[7]

11. A simple satisfaction survey with yes/no and multiple choice responses will not shed sufficient light on what people want and why.
      - Work with a professional survey designer to include open-ended

---

[7] See *TIPS for Conducting CITIZEN SURVEYS to Develop Government Performance Measures and Reports*, National Center for Civic Innovation, 2008, www.fcny.org/cgp.

questions that elicit the reasons for the ratings people assign.

- We have observed several instances where governments have made erroneous assumptions about the reason for some poor ratings on surveys and then taken costly actions that didn't solve the reason for the poor ratings, sometimes making them worse.

- Conversely, we have observed some governments assuming that a good rating was due to a reason different from what the public had in mind, leading to a false sense of comfort on the part of the government.

- Elicit the public's views regarding their preferred way in which they would like to receive regular performance reports, their needs and expectations about the content and style of the report, its frequency and preferred dissemination modes.

12. Include carefully designed surveys in existing communications, notices, bills, etc. that are being sent to residents to gauge their opinions and points of view.

Reports

13. Do not rely on website dissemination exclusively to tell your story. Remember that everyone does not have a computer, nor is it likely that people will read every page of your report from your website. Consider a variety of ways to make your data/information and report available and accessible—low tech and high tech.

14. Align performance measures and reports with what the public has identified as important and meaningful to them.

15. Some people want summary information about services and performance, others want detail. Provide both, allowing those who want the detail to drill down.

16. Report good and bad news, explaining the reasons for both.

17. They must be succinct and tell a story in a way that means something to the public.

18. Consider breaking up your report into substantive areas, releasing them at different times throughout the year.

19. Consider language differences; enlist reliable volunteers or use computerized translation functions to communicate to diverse audiences.

20. Be sure you are presenting data that are accurate and timely, "without spin."

21. Presentation matters. Make it visually pleasing, easy to read.

22. Provide context and explanations.

Working in a Financial Crisis

23. Use the performance measures to get feedback about what services are not important to or not valued by the public.

24. Some Trailblazers report that performance measurement was helpful with forecasting the economic crisis and keeping an eye on leading indicators.

25. Use a budget game to inform the public about the choices and their implications.

26. Work to make sure that performance measurement/management is used and viewed as necessary to provide facts that help monitor how government is doing and what issues need to be addressed during the crisis.

27. Public feedback helps you measure public sentiment towards reductions in services and can provide useful suggestions and alternatives.

Measuring "Customer" Service and Satisfaction

28. Discuss in focus groups; identify key factors relevant to the public.

29. Use "secret shopper" observers to assess performance and provide feedback to employees.

30. Provide the public with opportunities to give anonymous feedback.

31. Incorporate public engagement standards into employee training programs, job descriptions and performance ratings.

32. Do not rely on ratings alone. Ask why respondents gave their ratings.

33. Be sure program managers are made aware of the public's feedback and are responsive to their needs.

Using Performance Measures to Manage and Improve Performance

34. Make this work part of a manager's evaluation process.

35. Link to daily operations.

36. Integrate with the budget.

37. Seek ongoing customer feedback.

38. Involve all levels of the organization including gatekeepers, the first persons the public encounters.

Changes in Administration and Support

39. Anticipate that this may happen.

40. Identify your champions.

41. As new elected officials come in, do an orientation for them about performance measures.

42. Create a legislator's handbook.

43. Make sure that performance reporting is embedded throughout the organization.

44. Keep it simple. Streamline the internal lingo.

45. Be sensitive to what the significant issues are for elected officials and provide them with information and feedback about it.

46. Encourage legislation that mandates this work.

Adapting Social Media

47. Test and use social media to broaden outreach to populations who prefer that form of communication.

Adapting New Technology

48. Stay abreast of technological developments that can help make publicly engaged governments more effective and efficient.

49. Consider interactive websites, better software for reporting data, imaginative "games" and other communication aids.

Seek Out What Other Places Are Doing

50. Adapt what works for you and moves you forward.

PART FOUR

Chapter 8

WHY SOME GOVERNMENTS DID NOT APPLY TO THE TRAILBLAZER PROGRAM

While most of the commentary and research reported here describe the governments and their leaders who chose to become part of the Trailblazer Program and what they accomplished, if the objective is to cultivate publicly engaged governments, part of this research must start to explore why some chose to undertake this initiative and others did not.

SURVEYING NON-TRAILBLAZERS

Since the inception of the Trailblazer Program, CGP maintained an expanding list containing email addresses of potential Trailblazer applicants all of whom were sent email announcements inviting them to apply to the Trailblazer Program[8]. Some told us they would apply but didn't. Some were referred to us by Trailblazers, members of selection panels, colleagues, experts in the field or were members of various government organizations with an interest in performance measurement and related matters. All told, the list contained 2,470 individuals who were working in local or county governments and were not part of the Trailblazer Program. This list was the "universe" from which we sought information about the Non-Trailblazers group, seeking differences and similarities between them and Trailblazer participants. We received 69 responses.

---

[8] *Announcements about the program were made at national and local conferences, in hand-outs and newsletters of national organizations and their local chapters, and by word of mouth. It is likely that people learned of the program from several different sources.*

We designed an online survey, which sought to yield information in five different areas:

- Descriptive facts about the responding employee and government
- Current performance measurement and reporting practices
- Familiarity with the Government Trailblazer Program
- Reasons why their government did not apply; and
- Questions about innovation in government that attempt to establish the government's history and inclination toward new ideas and practices.

While some multiple-choice questions were provided to gain information in a quantitative form, the survey also used an open-ended answer format to give respondents the ability to comment and explain their answers.

COMPARING NON-TRAILBLAZERS TO TRAILBLAZERS

Similarity in the number of Trailblazers (70) and the number responding to the Non-Trailblazer survey (69) enable easy comparative analyses. Exhibits 12-15 point to wide geographical dispersion in both groups, although the Non-Trailblazer group has only one representative from the northeast. Trailblazers were in places with larger populations and, as to be expected, their operating budgets are larger as well. Most Non-Trailblazers governments were cities, while some were counties. However, there are no striking differences in geography, budget or type of government that, on their own, may account for the "to be or not to be" choice of becoming a Trailblazer.

Exhibit 12: Location of Trailblazer and Non-Trailblazer Governments

Region	Trailblazers	Non-Trailblazers
West	14	23
Midwest	12	19
Southwest	6	9
Southeast	20	15
Northeast	12	1
Canada	6	0
NA	-	1
Total	70	68

Sources: Center on Government Performance's Survey of Non-Trailblazers;
Trailblazer Applications 2003-2010
Among the responses were two from different people in the same government;
therefore information for 68 governments is presented here.

Exhibit 13: Population, Trailblazer and Non-Trailblazer Governments

Population	Trailblazers	Non-Trailblazers
Over 1 million	7	4
500,0000 to 1 million	7	6
100,000 to 499,999	27	15
25,000 to 99,999	16	21
Under 25,000	7	21
NA/NR (Not Relevant)	6	1
Total	70	68

Sources: Center on Government Performance's Survey of Non-Trailblazers;
Trailblazer Applications 2003-2010
Among the responses were two from different people in the same government;
therefore information for 68 governments is presented here.

Exhibit 14: Operating Budgets of Trailblazer and Non-Trailblazer Governments

Budget	Trailblazers	Non-Trailblazers
$1 Billion or more	12	8
$500 Million to $999.9 Million	14	6
$100 Million to $499.9 Million	23	17
$50 Million to $99.9 Million	8	10
$25 Million to $49.9 Million	4	12
Under $25 Million	9	12
NA	0	3
Total	70	68

Sources: Center on Government Performance's Survey of Non-Trailblazers;
Trailblazer Applications 2003-2010
Among the responses were two from different people in the same government;
therefore information for 68 governments is presented here.

Exhibit 15: Type of Government, Trailblazers and Non-Trailblazers

Type of Government	Trailblazers	Non-Trailblazers
City	39	48
Town	3	2
County	16	11
City-County	2	3
State & State-Wide Organizations	4	2
Special Governmental Entities	6	1
N/A	0	1
Total	70	68

Sources: Center on Government Performance's Survey of Non-Trailblazers;
Trailblazer Applications 2003-2010
Among the responses were two from different people in the same government;
therefore information for 68 governments is presented here.

WHAT NON-TRAILBLAZERS SAID

QUESTION: Are performance measures being produced for your government?

Of the 69 Non-Trailblazers who answered the question *"Are performance measures being produced for your government?"* 60 reported that they produce performance measures for all or some functions. [Exhibit 16] They would have met one of the criteria for applying to the Trailblazer Program.

Exhibit 16:

Are Performance Measures Being Produced for Non-Trailblazer Government Functions?	
All Functions	16
Some	44
None	9
Total	69

Sources: Center on Government Performance's Survey of Non-Trailblazers

QUESTION: Do you consult the public?

When asked if they consult the public about what kinds of performance measures and reports they would like to receive, 46 respondents reported that they did not. Of the 10 who answered "yes," the extent of public involvement they engaged in was not clear:

- Two acknowledged that they do not consult the public directly.
- Another has a citizen committee to help set high level goals for their strategic planning
- Three said they have surveys but did not describe the questions or purposes.
- Two mentioned meetings, committees and board discussions.

- One reported that priorities are discussed throughout the year.
- One stated that "periodic focus groups provide opportunities to obtain consumer/rate payer feedback, including performance measures."

The activities described above by these 10 governments do not meet the standards of public consultation envisioned by the Trailblazer Program.

QUESTIONS: What do you see as the major obstacles to consulting the public? Why did you or your government not apply to the Trailblazer Program?

✓ **Current fiscal conditions argue against this initiative**

> *"This is something we may be able to do in the future, when we have more resources, including staff resources."*

> *"There may be interest but not enough resources."*

> *"...the stipend is generous....However, I didn't think we could afford a consultant...for the amount offered...[and] I would have a very difficult time securing any supplemental funds from our local government as this would likely have been viewed as an unnecessary expense at a time of fiscal constraint."*

✓ **Their appointed and elected officials are not interested in public involvement in these matters**

> *"City Manager not interested in consulting the public."*

> *"Not under the current City Manager. Perhaps in the future when he leaves (4-6 years down the road)."*

> *"Elected officials avoid public involvement in goal setting."*

✓ **Staff is opposed**

"Only if forced."

"Not part of our culture."

"We are doing some reporting now and there is a commitment to PM but there is no mechanism in place for public involvement and little appetite to create one."

✓ **The public has little to offer on the subject of performance measures or reporting**

"[There is a] lack of understanding and interest on the part of the public. Staff has a better understanding of measures and what we have the ability to measure given staffing levels and budget constraints."

"No interest on the part of the public; resource constraints."

"Public not educated enough."

"Not sure what the public could offer other than opinion."

"'The public lacks a desire to engage on a broad scale with complicated decisions and prefers to see the elected officials making these tough decisions."

✓ **No relevant experience or knowledge**

"No prior experience involving the public."

"Do not know how to involve the public."

✓ **Fear of negative reactions**

> *"Could create negative opinions if we can't do what they want us to do."*

Trailblazer governments were confronted with the same daunting fiscal conditions as the Non-Trailblazer group. Many of the Trailblazers also had similar apprehensions about their ability to reach out to the public, fears about negative responses and doubts about whether the public would respond in helpful ways.

What is markedly different about Non-Trailblazers are two factors: (1) Their appointed and elected officials are not interested in initiating publicly engaged governing, and (2) the respondents themselves were not inclined to do this work. Therefore, unlike some Trailblazer project directors, the Non-Trailblazers were not inclined to take on the challenge of convincing their top management to move toward publicly engaged governments.

QUESTION: What conditions are necessary to launch and sustain an initiative?

Non-Trailblazers recognize the importance of leadership support. They said:

> *"Senior leaders with the capacity to afford, reward and support change."*

> *"Effective leadership. A progressive community."*

> *"Willing leadership, available staff and other resources; elected champion, citizens that trust their local government."*

> *"Leaders that support the initiative and hold their staff accountable for implementation."*

> *"A welcoming attitude of ideas from the top."*

"Motivated managers who believe they have an obligation to the citizens."

"Willing leadership; a defined need."

"Support from the highest level of senior management and the courage among his/her direct reports to carry that support down into the organization."

"Strong leader that is organized, firm."

"Leadership that encourages long-range planning and a team effort by all divisions within the government."

"Leadership which holds management responsible and accountable, but also wants them to understand and also become champions."

"Leadership support; adequate resources."

"Leadership support and good communication."

Non-Trailblazer respondents did not rule out eventually adopting a Trailblazer initiative, but set their own conditions:

"Willing to consider innovations, with documentation of cost savings or improvements in efficiency, provided that the investment isn't too great."

"Willing to implement if it makes sense and there are benefits."

"We are always looking for ways to improve what we do. While we haven't yet brought the public to the table in terms of defining measures, report characteristics, etc., I can see that being of value. Honestly, I think it could

be a while as we are struggling just to maintain the currently developed PM system we have in place. I think ultimately, we will develop a public report and then seek feedback on that report, rather than seeking feedback prior to giving a report."

"We are moving towards more citizen engagement, but right now that's focused on the vision/planning piece. We may move to measures, but that's in the future."

"As with all entities, there are always those that are resistant to new things; we are no different. I do believe with a little perseverance, this can be overcome."

[In our government, we would need]:
"Attitude adjustments."
"Increased awareness of the importance of public involvement in the development of performance measures and reports."
"Change in elected officials."

***

In the chapter on "Trailblazers and Innovation," we present a contrasting set of attitudes and conditions that typified Trailblazers, which helps explain how it is that they became innovators in their governments.

PART FIVE

Chapter 9

WHY THE TRAILBLAZER PROGRAM WORKED

By the end of their first year, practically all governments participating in the Trailblazer Program were able to reach out to the public to learn how the public judges government performance and how they want information reported. Participating governments then began acting on those findings. All but two Trailblazer governments have been or are about to be recipients of our certificates of completion awards. This is a remarkable achievement for a program that was experimental and challenging to governmental organizations facing large losses in revenue and staff and abounding criticism by many in the political debates of our time.

Many of the critics call for changes in the way governments do their business. A common opinion about government is that, for a variety of reasons, governments are loathe to change and adopt new ways. The fact that the Trailblazer Program successfully encouraged innovation primarily in local and county governments raises the question of what made this program work. In response, we call attention to several factors.

The collaboration and partnership of two organizations outside government with the 70 Trailblazer governments made this initiative possible. There were no hidden agendas, just a pure dedication to the purposes of the program.

The Trailblazer Program was encouraged by and funded primarily and for its entire eight years by the Alfred P. Sloan Foundation as part of its "Making Municipal Governments More Responsive to their Citizens" program. The Center on Government Performance (CGP), which conceived of and operated the Government

Trailblazer Program, has been part of the nonprofit, nonpolitical National Center for Civic Innovation (NCCI) and its sister organization, the Fund for the City of New York (FCNY). FCNY has a long history of helping local government measure and improve performance, often through introducing new technology. Its Board of Directors provided funds to supplement grants to some Trailblazer governments.

CGP and its staff brought to the Trailblazer Program extensive experience in working in government and sensitivity to the needs of government managers and executives as they conceive, develop and implement innovations. During the Trailblazer Program, CGP serves as its program director, manager, catalyst, facilitator, colleague, cheerleader, monitor and reporter/recorder—always urging the government representatives to keep going and do more and better in the interest of serving the public.

Some governments asked if membership and membership fees would be required, or if CGP, NCCI or FCNY would expect to serve as paid consultants to the Trailblazers, once selected; or they looked for some other "catch." There is and was no expectation or stated or unstated obligation other than for the Trailblazer governments to do their best to meet the program's requirements and implement publicly engaged governance. We think that the joining together of the aforementioned organizations for the sole purpose of initiating and operating this Trailblazer Program accounts for the respect it has earned and the extraordinary achievements of the Trailblazer governments and their representatives who volunteered to participate in this innovation.

PROVIDING ENCOURAGEMENT AND BEYOND

Managing large government operations and resources is a difficult job and a lonely one. The public sector offers few avenues for those rising in the government bureaucracies or for newcomers to share ideas and practices and learn new ones in an environment that is sensitive to and respectful of their positions. CGP provided that environment and a challenging one as well, setting forth clear objectives and deadlines and encouragement to do more, along with stimulating agendas and many chances for the exchange of information, counsel, ideas and ways to embolden one another.

   ✓   **Convening Trailblazers in a setting devoted entirely to this initiative was a central element in the Trailblazer Program's success.**

> *"With this group, there is a healthy competitiveness, since if one government is doing something great, others believe they can do it too. This way, we don't settle for 'good enough' and continuously improve."* (City project director)

> *"The inspiration garnered from NCCI/CGP and other Trailblazers is very helpful to moving ahead. It's useful to point at what others are doing and say, 'we need to do that here'."* (City program director)

> *"Talking with other communities is always encouraging and motivates me to try and push my organization to the next level. It encourages me to try and convince my organization to step out of its comfort zone."* (City budget and performance manager)

> *"Making the connections with other innovators helps to keep me on track and to keep my mind on the bigger vision if it is possible, and it serves to keep us always trying to improve upon what we have done."* (Project director)

> *"It has been invaluable to gather with the other Trailblazers and learn what they are up to and hear of best practices from around the world."* (City program director)

> *"The primary thing from reading PM reports from numerous jurisdictions and seeing the websites of places like King County, Vancouver, Nashville,*

etc., is just realizing what is possible—especially the interactive websites. What we now see as our ultimate goal for reporting PM to citizens is beyond what we imagined when we applied for the grant." (County budget/finance analyst)

"Lots of ideas from others and a sense of family! There was always something to learn from others and someone with which you could share something that would help them." [City performance analyst]

"Based upon information learned during the 2008 Trailblazer Conference about how other communities had structured their performance measurement programs, I established a formalized structure for our own." (City executive)

"It is nice to not have to 'reinvent the wheel'." (City budget/finance analyst)

"[I like the] cross connection to the other practitioners... and I appreciate learning about shared challenges and approaches with a practical perspective." (County executive)

"Gathering with other Trailblazers is inspirational and informational. These gatherings recognize this work. It's great to learn from others and figure out what would be next steps for us." (City program director)

✓ **The small grants, seemingly insignificant in a government's large budget, made a significant difference.**

"With the Trailblazer grant, [we were] able to acquire materials that would be unobtainable during the current fiscal environment. This grant also

made [our government] think beyond its limitations and look for new ways
to promote future reports." (City performance analyst)

"Before this grant was awarded, there were no performance measures
in place. This grant was the spark needed for this organization to get a
performance management program in place." (City executive)

"Now, the current practice has been modified [from reporting on ICMA
(International City/County Management Association) measures only]
to incorporate citizen feedback about existing measures and creation of
new measures for every department. Citizen feedback is collected via
focus groups and surveys. This change in process is a direct result of the
[CGP] grant, which paid for the first round of focus groups and allowed
departments to see the value of citizen feedback and interest in performance
measurement." (City planning director)

"We had started down this path prior to being involved; I think this
program significantly accelerated our progress with the recognition it
brought, and the money allowed us to experiment with our outreach in
ways we would not have." (City performance analyst)

"Because of the funding from the NCCI/CGP .... An expectation now
exists to see what has become of the annual performance report. The
narrative comes from the department heads, the City Manager and
the Mayor. Much of the data are collected for the budget and/or the
Performance Measurement Project. We produce the mock-up in-house and
outsource the design, layout and printing. It's a team effort. I requested
and received some funding for this in the FY-07 budget." (City budget/
finance analyst)

✓   **The work, as it was being accomplished, provided Trailblazer project directors with a deep sense of pride and satisfaction.**

"It's great to be part of the Trailblazer Program because it inspires, challenges, and reminds us to continue the work of improvement." (County analyst)

"We conducted the three focus groups specifically to address two items: excellent customer service and the content, format and layout of the performance report. This exercise was among the most valuable experiences that I have had in my professional life." (City budget/finance analyst)

"Seeing our First Annual Performance Report made me very proud, but having the opportunity to hear the honest, uninhibited feedback of our citizens, knowing I had the ability to respond to their suggestions made me the most proud." (City budget/finance analyst)

"It is a great help to continue to be part of the Trailblazer group or cohort, because it inspires, challenges and reminds us to continue the work of improvement, even when our organizational environment might not always be conducive to continuous improvement in these areas." (County analyst)

Chapter 10

SOME THOUGHTS ABOUT THE FUTURE: MOVING TOWARD PUBLICLY ENGAGED GOVERNING

The hope for this program and some others funded by the Alfred P. Sloan Foundation under its "Making Municipal Governments More Responsive to their Citizens" program has been to institutionalize local governments' practices of being more responsive to the needs of the public, aligning government activities with the public's perspectives and producing timely and full information on a regular basis about government activities and operations in ways that are accessible and understandable to the public. Our Trailblazer Program has helped 70 local governments start up these initiatives and reap benefits from them.

The path toward achieving the objectives we set out for the Trailblazers was not smooth or in a straight line. We have seen some ups and downs in support from the top levels of their governments, trials and errors, interruptions—some long-lasting—in some places, then surprising spurts of new achievements and great success in others. Each city and county government is different—its progress unpredictable.

Some governments now have embodied in their laws, a requirement that performance reporting be conducted on a regular basis. One city, thanks to a Trailblazer's efforts, now has a legal requirement that the public be consulted about the performance measures that are to be used!

As for those without legal mandates, the question remains whether these publicly engaged government programs will continue to have the support to sustain and expand. Some Trailblazers have every expectation that they will.

"I believe that, primarily on the reporting side, we will increasingly look to the citizens to guide the program. Certainly, we will continue to collect and analyze a considerable amount of performance data that we believe to be essential but that our citizens have little interest in. However, our regular reporting to the public will be guided by what they tell us is important to them. My hope is that this trend toward increased citizen involvement in the decision-making process will spill into other areas of our operations and result in a more engaged citizenry." (City executive)

"Our City Manager approved, shortly after my return from NY and discussing with him, adding a person to my staff who will work half time on Performance Reporting in addition to assigning half a person from Finance. This will allow the report to be produced and even expanded in the future." (City budget/finance/audit officer)

"They (performance measures) are used extensively in discussions with departments and very much a part of our budget development culture." (City performance manager)

"This initiative has spurred changes in the way programs are being managed in that the business planning process is now inclusive of performance measurements." (City executive)

THERE IS MUCH WORK STILL TO BE DONE

We need to address the conditions that cause the Non-Trailblazers to shy away from this new program, even though it offered unusual support and benefits. Respondents reported that some of their government leaders were not interested in listening to and learning from the public. Organizations that serve the interests of mayors, county executives and city managers may find the results of our survey of interest to them since surely they are concerned about improving the public's perception of government and government employees. The reluctance to make changes and take some risks are understandable but surely are necessary in this fast-changing environment in which the public demands and needs information and technology provides seemingly never-ending ways to obtain it, quickly and easily.

Similarly, both degree-granting and continuing education programs in our schools of public policy, government, public management, public administration and related fields play critical roles in inspiring their enrollees to take on new initiatives, learn from other jurisdictions and introduce new ideas and practices. Some of our most effective Trailblazers were motivated to take on this program shortly after completing their graduate studies.

Governments themselves run or support training, management development and executive development programs for their employees. If the curriculum were to include increasing employees' understanding and sensitivity to the issues involved in introducing and sustaining innovations in their government and the practices involved in publicly engaged governing, perhaps the Non-Trailblazers will feel more inclined to take on the new challenges they will face. Among the skills and information they need are practice with effective methods of reaching out and listening to the public; the significance of aligning the public's needs with government services; honing skills in preparing and disseminating clear information to their public; effective, respectful ways to communicate with the public and ways in which performance measures and reports can help them manage, set standards for their employees and improve government services and productivity.

WHAT TRAILBLAZERS WANT

Trailblazers want the Trailblazer Program and their participation to continue.

✓ **Meetings are vital.** Trailblazers have expressed hopes that we continue annual meetings for them. We know that the bonds they form and the lessons they learn from one another in our sessions with them are powerful, efficient, inspiring and sustaining influences.

"I think that these meeting over the years have sustained my interest and passion for listening to the public and incorporating citizen needs with all aspects of government. Somehow, continuing these annual meetings, meeting new people and hearing firsthand what people are doing would be extremely valuable." (City performance manager)

"Meeting with colleagues once per year to exchange ideas is invaluable. I would request money in our budget to attend and annual Trailblazer meeting if the CGP was unable to cover my travel costs. The probability that my request would be honored is unknowable at this time." (City budget/finance analyst)

"Would love for these Trailblazer conferences to continue. They have been so beneficial in providing me with ideas on how to handle/address multiple issues with citizens/elected officials and executive management." (Project director)

✓ **Trailblazers think the Center on Government Performance's continuing role is essential**

"Without your inspiration and support it is doubtful that the 70 Trailblazer local government jurisdictions would have undertaken the daunting task to: 'Reach out to their public in new, non-confrontational ways, listen to what measures they use and what information they want and need from government … And to incorporate, whenever possible, the public perspective into their performance measures, reports and management practices.'" (County performance manager)

"Your publications and gatherings of Trailblazers are very critical to assisting Trailblazers on this journey." (City program director)

"Continue to help us network nationally. This opportunity has helped us show skeptical departments that we aren't alone in asking people to measure. Accountability and using data to help make decisions is here to stay. Offering opportunities or serving as a resource to help share knowledge in this area would be great." (County analyst)

"[Your continuing] to provide leadership in this area would be helpful. With changes in government, priorities can shift or change, and CGP as a driving force offers hope that if it does lose momentum it can be gained again or shown as an opportunity of what's happening nationally." (County performance manager)

[I would like the Trailblazer program to] *"1. Keep the listserv/group together, 2. Make announcements to the group about Trailblazers trying new innovative approaches, 3. Keep us on track with citizen input being the focus; it is very easy to get too focused on what we do."* (City management and budget analyst)

"Continue to keep the group in touch and communicating with one another...." (County budget/finance/audit officer)

"[We need] continuous reminders of the importance of this work, including success stories and how folks have overcome challenges." (Project director)

AFTERWORD

We need innovation and innovators in government. Dwindling fiscal resources and other pressures facing local and county governments require new approaches, energy and commitment to public service. The need for the public to have confidence in its government is undeniable in a democracy.

The Trailblazer Program emphasizes innovations to bring government and the public together to share information and points of view in ways that lead to greater understanding and improved performance.

We have seen that when people learn why government does some of the things it does, understanding replaces skepticism, anger and misunderstandings. Understanding can also lead to a more active citizenry and greater public-government collaborations.

Similarly, when governments learn how the public perceives of their work and what the public needs in the way of information and actions to help them through their daily lives, and when government learns how much the public needs and depends on government, governments are inclined to respond positively, whenever possible, to the public's needs and suggestions.

Trailblazers doing this work need support and encouragement to continue these essential undertakings. They need support and encouragement from foundations, nonprofits, universities, professional organizations and publications that serve government, and from government itself. Government Trailblazer work needs to be an ongoing venture. We need more Trailblazers!

ACKNOWLEDGEMENTS

The Center on Government Performance started in the Fund for the City of New York and has worked within it and its sister organization, the National Center for Civic Innovation, since 1995. The support of its President, Dr. Mary McCormick, members of the Board and staff has been essential to the Center's growth and sustenance. We are grateful for their many forms of generosity and wise counsel.

All the work of the Center on Government Performance was encouraged and funded by the Alfred P. Sloan Foundation. Words cannot adequately express our appreciation for their intellectual and financial support. We are especially grateful to the Foundation's two presidents—Dr. Ralph Gomory who conceived of and expanded their Making Municipal Governments More Responsive to Their Citizens program, and Dr. Paul Joskow for helping us continue our work through the phases of the Trailblazer Program reported here. Dr. Ted Greenwood has been our Program Officer there for most of the Center's life. He has rendered critiques, suggestions and ideas that have helped guide our Center's work. We have shared many exchanges about how, in the Sloan Foundation's words, "to make citizen-informed and citizen-based government performance measurement and reporting widespread, normal and expected." He has been a partner at presentations we both have made at national meetings. And he has moved forward the implementation of his foundation's vision with great energy and determination.

This volume was produced and the entire Government Trailblazer Program ran so well because of the devoted and skilled staff of the Center on Government Performance. Of the current and former staff who worked on this project:

Nancy Allendorf held the position of Program Officer for this program. She kept track of each Trailblazer's progress, managed the awarding of their grants and reimbursements, and supervised the logistics for five annual Trailblazer meetings. She pored through their reports, extracting data for possible inclusion here. She also monitored our month-to-month financial status.

Rick Bruner designed the Trailblazer map, posters for seven Trailblazer meetings, the covers and style for the agendas for all of them, designed the "look" of our scores of presentations and was our photographer at Trailblazer meetings.

Verna Vasquez, Associate Director of the Center, oversaw staff assignments for this lengthy initiative. She set up the administrative systems—starting with the original demonstration grant—to monitor the Trailblazers' work, designed the application form, was involved in the selection processes, helped start our Trailblazer listserv, worked on the agendas for Trailblazer meetings, attended all of them and helped with the many presentations we made around the country about this program. She has read through every word of every draft of this book. In short, she has been involved in all the steps along the way, always at the ready to do more, and suggest how we can do more and better. She is an extraordinary talent and treasured colleague.

Harriet Gianoulis runs our ComNET (Computerized Neighborhood Environment Tracking) Program which was adopted by several Trailblazer cities that wanted to work in new ways with their local residents to identify street level conditions and exchange ideas about how and what could be done to correct them. ComNET is a remarkably effective civic engagement tool that fed directly into the Trailblazer Program's purposes. And Harriet is a remarkably talented programmer, technologist, trainer and colleague.

Bill Huggins, the newest member of the staff jumped right in to help us find out who the Non-Trailblazers are. He researched the email announcement lists, helped draft and monitored the online questionnaire, gathered the results and provided drafts of findings. He quickly mastered Survey Monkey and Constant Contact for our purposes. He also did initial research on innovation, and manages much of our administrative records and functions. He is a smart researcher and wordsmith. We have him to thank for coming up with the term "publicly engaged governing" as a substitute for a longer tongue-twister. He is an energetic, willing, enthusiastic and helpful addition to our group.

The Governmental Accounting Standards Board, under the leadership of Robert Attmore helped start the demonstration grant program which later transformed into the Government Trailblazer Program. Jay Fountain and Wilson Campbell there provided wise advice and encouragement during the early days of reviewing applications and selecting participants. We consulted many other leaders in the field to help screen applications, as well.

Ned Steele, MediaImpact's president, read through every page of this manuscript. As he did for the *Listening to the Public* book, he provided thoughtful suggestions and comments directed always toward making clear the messages embodied in the Center's and the Trailblazers' work and accomplishments. If there are any failures in the way I have told this story, they are mine and surely, not his. His understanding, patience, generosity with his time during an already overstretched schedule and his helpfulness cannot be overstated.

The most resounding kudos must go to the Trailblazer directors from around the U.S. and Canada. In one way or another, they helped move the work forward in their government. Their roles varied. Some were the leaders of the Trailblazer effort from beginning to end. They took risks, worked long hours, sweated out uncertainties, kept in good humor, cheered on other Trailblazers and us and became successful innovators under the most trying circumstances, connecting their governments with the people they serve. Others substituted or filled in. The public may not know their names, but we know that the public in their cities, towns, counties, states and provinces are better off because of the Trailblazers' dedication and commitment to public service.

It has been an enormous privilege to work with all those mentioned above.

Barbara J. Cohn Berman
Director
Center on Government Performance
Vice President
National Center for Civic Innovation

Innovation in Organizations: Selected References

Altshuler, Alan. "Bureaucratic Innovation, Democratic Accountability and Political Incentives." *Innovation In American Government: Challenges, Opportunities, and Dilemmas.* Eds. Alan Altshuler and Robert Behn. Washington D.C.: Brooking Institution Press, 1997. 38-67.

Bacon, Nicola, Nusrat Faizullah, Geoff Mulgan, and Saffron Woodcraft. "Transformers: How Local Areas Innovate to Address Changing Social Needs." NESTA (2008).

Behn, Robert. "The Dilemmas of Innovation in American Government." *Innovation In American Government: Challenges, Opportunities, and Dilemmas.* Eds. Alan Altshuler and Robert Behn. Washington D.C.: Brooking Institution Press, 1997. 3-37.

Behn, Robert. "Do Goals Help Create Innovative Organizations?" *Public Management Reform and Innovation: Research Theory, and Application.* Eds. George Frederickson and Jocelyn Johnston. Tuscaloosa: The University of Alabama Press, 1999. 79-88.

Behn, Robert. "Why Measure Performance? Different Purposes Require Different Measures." *Public Administration Review* 63.5 (2003): 586-606.

Bennis, Warren. "Why Leaders Can't Lead." *Life in Organizations: Workplaces As People Experience Them.* Eds. Rosabeth Kanter and Barry Stein. New York: Basic Books Inc., 1979. 36-48.

Bingham, Richard. "Innovation, Bureaucracy, and Public Policy: A Study of Innovation Adoption by Local Government." *The Western Political Quarterly* 31.2 (1978): 178-205.

Burt, Ronald. "Structural Holes and Good Ideas." *The American Journal of Sociology* 110.2 (2004): 349-399.

Cavalluzzo, Ken, and Christopher Ittner. "Implementing Performance Measurement Innovation: Evidence from Government." *Accounting, Organizations and Society* 29 (2004): 243-267.

CCAF-FCVI. "Innovation, Risk & Control" Ottawa: CCAF-FCVI Inc. (2010).

Costanza, Robert. "Visions of Alternative (Unpredictable) Futures and Their Use in Policy Analysis." Conservation Ecology 4.1 (2000). 28 Feb. 2000. <http://www.consecol.org/vol4/iss1/art5/>

REFERENCES

Colvin, Geoff. *Talent Is Overrated: What Really Separates World-Class Performers from Everybody Else.* New York: The Penguin Group, 2008.

Davis, Mike. "Building Innovative Bureaucracies: Change, Structure, and the Science of Ideas." *The Public Manager* 32.4 (2003): 3-6.

Dometrius, Nelson, Deil Wright and Nathan Mitchell. "Innovativeness as a Trait of American States: Does it Exist?" Paper presented at the Annual Meeting of the American Political Science Association. Philadelphia, August 2006.

Drucker, Peter. *Innovation and Entrepreneurship: Practice and Principles.* New York: Harper & Row Publishers, 1985.

Dyer, Jeff, Hal Gregersen, and Clayton Christensen. *The Innovator's DNA: Mastering the Five Skills of Disruptive Innovators.* Boston: Harvard Business Review Press, 2011.

Fullan, Michael. "The Challenge of Change: Start School Improvement Now!" Thousand Oaks: Corwin Press, 2009.

Hannah, Susan. "The Correlates of Innovation: Lessons from Best Practice." *Public Productivity & Management Review* 19.2 (1995): 216-228.

Haveri, Arto. "Complexity in Local Government Change." *Public Management Review* 8.1 (2006): 31-46.

Hill, Susan. "Team Leadership." *Leadership: Theory and Practice.* Ed. Peter Northhouse. Thousand Oaks: Sage, 2007. 207-236.

Gilroy, Leonard. "Innovators in Government Offer Cutting-Edge Models of Reform." *The Reason Foundation.* 28 Sept. 2008. Web. 8 Feb. 2010. <http://reason.org/news/show/innovators-in-government-offer>

Golden, Olivia. "Innovation in Public Sector Human Services Programs: The Implications of Innovation by 'Groping Along'." *Innovation In American Government: Challenges, Opportunities, and Dilemmas.* Eds. Alan Altshuler and Robert Behn. Washington D.C.: Brooking Institution Press, 1997. 146-174.

Gregersen, Hal. "The Innovator's DNA" *Insead Knowledge* 21 Dec. 2009. Web. 21 Jan. 2010. <http://knowledge.insead.edu/innovation-innovators-dna-091221.cfm?vid=358>

Kanter, Rosabeth. *The Change Masters: Innovation & Entrepreneurship in the American Corporation.* New York: Simon and Schuster, 1984.

Kee, James, and Kathryn Newcomer. "Why Do Change Efforts Fail? What Can Leaders Do About It?" *The Public Manager* 37.3 (2008): 5-12.

Lynn Jr., Laurence. "Innovation and the Public Interest: Insights from the Private Sector." *Innovation In American Government: Challenges, Opportunities, and Dilemmas.* Eds. Alan Altshuler and Robert Behn. Washington D.C.: Brooking Institution Press, 1997. 83-103.

McNabb, David. *The New Face of Government: How Public Managers Are Forging a New Approach to Governance.* Boca Raton: CRC Press, 2009.

Mintrom, Michael. "Policy Entrepreneurs and the Diffusion of Innovation." *American Journal of Political Science.* 41.3 (1997): 738-770.

Miron, Ella, Miriam Erez, and Eitan Naveh. "Do Personal Characteristics and Cultural Values That Promote Innovation, Quality, and Efficiency Compete or Complement Each Other?" *Journal of Organization Behavior* 25.2 (2004): 175-199.

Neff, Gina. "The Constitution of Innovative Industries: Networking Events and the Formation of the Internet Industry." Paper presented at the Annual Meeting of the American Sociological Association. San Francisco, August 2004.

Oakley, Kate, Brooke Sperry, and Andy Pratt. "The Art of Innovation: How Fine Arts Graduates Contribute to Innovation." Ed. Hasan Bakhshi. NESTA (2008).

Osborne, David, and Ted Gaebler. *Reinventing Government: How the Entrepreneurial Spirit Is Transforming the Public Sector.* Reading: Addison-Wesley, 1992.

Osborne, David, and Peter Plastrik. *Banishing Bureaucracy: The Five Strategies for Reinventing Government.* New York: Penguin Group, 1998.

Osborne, David. "Reinventing Government: What A Difference A Strategy Makes." Presented at 7th Global Forum on Reinventing Government: Building Trust in Government. Vienna, Austria, June 2007.

Patterson, Fiona, Maura Kerrin, Geraldine Gatto-Roissard, and Phillipa Coan. "Everyday Innovation: How to enhance innovative working in employees and organisations." NESTA (2009).

Rogers, Everett. *Diffusion of Innovations.* 4th ed. New York: The Free Press, 1995.

Schachter, Hindy. *Reinventing Government or Reinventing Ourselves*. Albany: State University of New York Press, 1997.

Schneider, Mark, Paul Teske, and Michael Mintrom. *Public Entrepreneurs: Agents for Change in American Government*. Princeton: Princeton University Press, 1995.

Schroeder, Roger, Andrew Van de Ven, and Gary Scudder. "The Development of Innovation Ideas." *Research on the Management of Innovation: The Minnesota Studies*. Eds. Andrew Van de Ven, Harold Angle, Marshall Poole. New York: Oxford University Press, 2000. 107-134.

Slavin, Adam, and Joan Woodard. *Enterprise Transformation: Lessons Learned, Pathways to Success*. Sandia National Laboratories, 2006.

"Trade-Off Time: How Four States Continue to Deliver." Pew Center on the States (2009).

Verganti, Roberto. *Design-Driven Innovation: Changing the Rules of Competition by Radically Innovating What Things Mean*. Boston: Harvard Business Press, 2009.

Weber, Max. *"Science as a Vocation." From Max Weber: Essays in Sociology*. Trans. and Eds. Hans Gerth and C. Wright Mills. New York: Oxford University Press, 1946. 129-156.

Wolman, Harold. "Innovators in Local Government and Fiscal Austerity." *Journal of Public Policy:* 6.2 (1986): 159-180.

Barbara J. Cohn Berman, recipient of the Harry Hatry Distinguished Performance Measurement Practice Award from the American Society for Public Administration, has been breaking new ground since 1995 by introducing the public's voice to government performance measurement, reporting and management.

She has been invited to make presentations throughout the U.S., in the United Kingdom, Canada and in Australia about her work on publicly engaged governing. She has served on many boards and advisory committees, including a task force of the Governmental Accounting Standards Board and was a member of the National Performance Management Advisory Commission. In addition to editing a special issue of the *National Civic Review* and contributing to journals, professional publications and textbooks, she is the author of *Listening to the Public: Adding the Voices of the People to Government Performance Measurement and Reporting*, the companion book to this volume, and of two volumes of a study, *How Smooth Are New York City's Streets?*

Ms. Cohn Berman served in several New York City administrations as deputy and assistant commissioners in housing and personnel development, where she introduced innovative practices and programs and linked performance measures with productivity improvements. She helped design and oversaw major urban research. She is the founding director of the Center on Government Performance in the National Center for Civic Innovation and its sister organization, the Fund for the City of New York. She has taught graduate courses in public policy and public administration, and was a Loeb Fellow at Harvard University.

National Center for Civic Innovation
is an Affiliate of the Fund for the City of New York
Center on Government Performance
121 Avenue of the Americas
New York, NY 10013
212-925-6675
www.civicinnovation.org
www.fcny.org

"Seeing our First Annual Performance Report made me very proud, but having the opportunity to hear the honest, uninhibited feedback of our citizens, knowing I had the ability to respond to their suggestions made me the most proud." (City budget/finance analyst)

"It is good to know that the public is interested in us. They helped us recognize that we have been collecting some data needlessly. [We learned that] all encounters with the public do not have to be confrontational." (Project director)

"After working our performance measures for 20+ years, I realized we were not reporting information which decisions could be made on. I decided we needed to change the style of measures we produce." (City director)

www.ingramcontent.com/pod-product-compliance
Lightning Source LLC
Chambersburg PA
CBHW081419270326
41931CB00015B/3327